DATING
A NARCISSIST

The brutal truth you don't want to hear

How to spot a narcissist on the very first date and set boundaries to become psychopath free

Dr. Theresa J. Covert

© Copyright 2019 - All rights reserved.

The content contained within this book may not be reproduced, duplicated, or transmitted without direct written permission from the author or the publisher.

Under no circumstances will any blame or legal responsibility be held against the publisher, or author, for any damages, reparation, or monetary loss due to the information contained within this book; either directly or indirectly.

Legal Notice:

This book is copyright protected. This book is only for personal use. You cannot amend, distribute, sell, use, quote or paraphrase any part, or the content within this book, without the consent of the author or publisher.

Disclaimer Notice:

Please note the information contained within this document is for educational and entertainment purposes only. All effort has been executed to present accurate, up to date, and reliable, complete information. No warranties of any kind are declared or implied. Readers acknowledge that the author is not engaging in the rendering of legal, financial, medical, or professional advice.

Table of Contents

Introduction 5
The Three Cycles of Narcissistic Abuse 11
    Chapter 1 Love Bombing - Why Do Narcissists Seem So Perfect? 12
    Chapter 2 Devaluation – Honeymoon's Over! 18
    Chapter 3 Discarding – Run Away and Never Look Back 26
Narcissistic Manipulation In Dating 32
    Chapter 4 The Overt Narcissist and The Covert Narcissist 33
    Chapter 5 The Narcissist's Harem 44
    Chapter 6 They will HOOVER you! 51
    Chapter 7 The Gaslighting Trick 58
    Chapter 8 Future Faking 64
    Chapter 9 Flying Monkeys 70
Dating The Narcissist 76
    Chapter 10 Do You Want to Know why You are Dating a Narcissist? 77
    Chapter 11 An Important Question - Am I Dating a Narcissist? 82
    Chapter 12 The Signs That You are Dating a Narcissist 90
    Chapter 13 Narcissistic Date Vs. Healthy Date 97

Chapter 14 Six Sneaky Things Narcissists Do to Get You Back 103
Chapter 15 LIES... 108
Chapter 16 Dating Tips... 116
Chapter 17 Healing After Dating a Narcissist........122
Chapter 18 Healthy Love – Dating After a Narcissist 128
Chapter 19 First Date – How to Spot a Narcissist. 135

Conclusion 141

Introduction

Nicole met Jones at a friend's party in October. They had not talked for an hour when Jones asked her out on a weekend date.

She said yes to dinner with Jones at a fancy restaurant. She said yes to another date with him; she couldn't resist this man.

Jones was charming. He would leave flowers at the office for Nicole. He texted her almost every minute of the day, and the never-ending gifts were a thing too. He showered Nicole with lots of attention.

Nicole felt unique to him.

In Nicole's eyes, Jones was the perfect partner. Nicole couldn't say no to Jones when he asked her to move in with him. She thought maybe she had finally found THE ONE.

However, things do not seem perfect of late; everything seems fine with Jones at work.

He was happy at the law firm where he worked, but Nicole found that they have been arguing much of late.

Also, Jones seems to be nitpicking at her. He used to love her hairstyle and the way she laughs; now he says she doesn't look real in her braids anymore, and she makes horrible sounds when she laughs.

Jones is never wrong even in the face of real facts now,

and she is now labeled as being dramatic.

She is the angry one now, she is the selfish one, and she is also the crazy one.

Nicole got tired of Jones' acts and wanted to move out, and so she tolds Jones about her plans, and suddenly Jones went on his knees to apologize to her.

Jones has been acting all sweet and affectionate again.

Dating can be expressed in light of two definitions. One, dating can be regarded as going on dates and getting out to actively meet people and spending time with them. Second, which is the focus of this book, dating is seeing someone specific regularly with an intention in mind, and with a purpose.

Dating can also be said to be a situation where two persons are attracted to each other.

Two people who like each other spend time together to see if they can stand each other for a long while.

If two people can stand to be around each other, they develop a relationship.

Dating is an attempt to determine compatibility; two people meet together and get around to know the things they like about each other and the things they don't.

When two persons spend time together to find a committed relationship with each other, they can be said to be dating each other. Dating is not seeing a person with other intentions such as business or a casual get to know.

Dating comes down to seeing a person with the possibility of having a future long term relationship with them.

In the search for a potential mate, there is a chance that you might land for yourself a narcissist. There is also a chance you might find someone healthy for yourself, but you must recognize a narcissist from the start before you fall hard in love with them.

Are you currently seeing someone with the hopes of establishing a serious relationship with them? It is also essential that you assess the person you are going out with now that things are just beginning to get serious.

There are narcissists everywhere: they are at the office, they are in the family, they are at schools.

Name anywhere people are, there is a chance that a narcissist is present. With the increasing presence of the internet today in our lives, narcissists can be found on social media websites and dating websites.

Dating mobile applications and social media have made it easy for people to connect faster than ever before. However, they bring downsides such as making it easy for narcissists to find victims at ease; these tools also make it easy for narcissists to manipulate people.

Narcissists find it easy to manipulate through social media platforms not only because of the ease of use of these platforms but also because it is not difficult to portray who you are not on social media.

Narcissists can sit in their couch and effortlessly keep on

swiping on profiles to find potential targets.

Apart from the possibility of an excellent future long-term relationship, there are also lots of benefits to dating a healthy person. Dating a healthy person can bring emotional benefits as well as physical health benefits.

Seeing someone has been shown by several studies to give a boost to happiness levels, and apart from promoting happiness, dating someone healthy has also been proven to reduce stress.

People in committed relationships have lower levels of the stress hormone, cortisol.

When a person is happy and has low stress hormone levels, they feel on top of the world, because being in a healthy relationship provides feelings of trust, support, and love in a person. Dating also helps to develop an individual's personality because people can learn how to handle situations and their relationships with other people.

Dating an unhealthy person comes with major downsides; the toxic partner may start to nitpick and always criticize the other partner. Dating an unhealthy person is like having a one-sided partnership; just a single person makes all big and small relationship decisions.

Apart from a decision making imbalance, an unhealthy partner will always place their needs above the needs of the relationship.

Narcissists can be charming and charismatic, which explains why people are often drawn to them. They are extremely likable people at first sight and are lovely people before they reveal their true colors.

They exhibit a pattern of abnormal behavior characterized by enlarged feelings of self-importance, an excessive need for admiration from others, and a general lack of understanding of the opinions of other people.

This book aims at providing information in an enlightening and entertaining way about how narcissists manipulate in the dating scene, and the not-too-talked-about downsides of being in an abusive relationship with a narcissist. It also brings into light the traits in people that makes them attractive to narcissists, the phases of dating with a narcissist and how narcissists seek to manipulate their partners.

Apart from that, it also discusses in details how narcissists operate in romantic relationships; love bombing, gaslighting, devaluing, discarding, and a host of other sneaky tactics. This book includes the ways of healing after narcissistic abuse and how not to fall victim to another relationship with a narcissist. It also focuses on the overt and the covert narcissists and how they operate in intimate relationships.

I wrote this to enlighten you about what a relationship with a narcissist looks like, and also to let you know that you can get through a bad relationship in case you have found yourself dating a narcissist.

Both men and women have fallen prey to narcissistic abuse, especially in intimate relationships, and this book views dating a narcissist from the two gender perspectives.

I hope to add to your previous knowledge about narcissists and narcissistic relationships, and also help you to recover and find your feet again if you happen to have been a victim of abuse.

Thanks for purchasing this. I hope that you find it enlightening and empowering as you come along with me.

The Three Cycles of Narcissistic Abuse

Chapter 1

Love Bombing - Why Do Narcissists Seem So Perfect?

It would be good to start the discussion about narcissistic abuse in dating with the stages narcissists go through with their victims. Narcissistic abuse is not always emotional; sometimes, it is physical or a combination of both.

Narcissists are manipulative and dangerous people who have a cycle they take their targets through, and they will perform some specific actions and say certain words to draw their victims in. These same facts are real for dating too, and love bombing is the very first phase of dating a narcissist.

Love bombing, also referred to as *idealization,* is the feeling of being swept away by a man or a woman. When you meet a new person who is totally into you, and the person showers you with the attention, and the validation you have always wanted, you naturally begin to think you have found the right person for you, especially when you are out trying to find love.

For the narcissist, this is the stage of the relationship when they put their deceptive mask on and pretend to be who they are not. It is the point where they present the best version of a healthy person as they can. They are caring, loving, and everything right a person might be. It is normal to shower a new love interest with attention and to be over the moon about them, but, when the attention feels excessive and obsessive, there could be a chance that your new-found partner might be using a tool of psychological manipulation called love bombing.

Love bombing is a tool a narcissist uses for manipulating by overwhelming the person with lots of love and affection. Love bombing occurs in cycles which are repeated over and over again by the narcissist.

Going back to the story of Nicole and Jones in the introduction of this book, we can see an excellent example of love bombing: Jones used love bombing to ensure that Nicole falls in love with him.

At the beginning of their relationship, Jones was all sweet and charming, constantly texting Nicole and sending her gifts frequently. While a narcissist might be a woman or a man, in most cases, women fall victim to love bombing because a majority of women are looking for the storybook fairytale kind of love. Narcissists will play according to this weakness right from the first minute of meeting their victims. The same goes for men who fall victim to narcissistic women, while they might not hold fairytales in their minds, the constant attention and the charming demeanor of the narcissistic woman might hook them in.

Now, let's move forward to the signs of love bombing in a relationship. The "love bombing" actions of a narcissist are not going to be the same in every situation, but there are a few signs common to all cases. It might be confusing to distinguish between what is a romantic gesture and love bombing in some cases. But an excellent way to spot the difference is waiting to see what happens next.

While if it is a romantic gesture, a healthy partner's words and actions are always consistent, whereas a love bombing narcissist will place their partner on a pedestal at first and knock them off later. The few telltale signs of a love bombing narcissist include but are not limited to: extravagant gifts, constant complimentary texting, mirroring behaviors, a strong push for intimacy, and obsessive flattery.

Flattery comes into the mix as soon as a narcissist meets someone new, and this flattery is not a one time kind of flattery, it keeps on coming and coming after the narcissist finds a new target. Obsessive flattery by the narcissist comes in the form of giving excessive, insincere praise.

Narcissists use flattery to get their victims addicted to the pleasure that comes from approval. Unknown to the victims, obsessive flattery is a love bombing tactic which the narcissist uses to learn more about the victim's insecurities and vulnerabilities.

With the advent of social media and instant messaging, narcissists in the early stages of dating their victims send long sappy messages. They are always checking up on the victim, sending love messages, good morning messages, good evening messages, good night messages, etc.

Bombarding the victim with long messages is a love-bombing technique aimed at making the victim feel special and associating the feeling of being exclusive with the narcissist.

Mirroring behavior is another way narcissists love bomb their victims; every action of the victim is reflected by the narcissist, apart from imitating the practices of the victim, narcissists will pretend to have similar interests with the victim. If the victim loves to play basketball, the narcissist loves to play basketball too. If the victim loves to swim, the narcissist loves to swim also.

In the love-bombing phase, narcissists say they have fallen in love with their victims; they say they are loyal and push for sex and intimacy early on in the relationship. The ultimate goal of the narcissist using love bombing is to make the victim dependent on them very early in the relationship. Extravagant gifts that come in the line of the victims' interests are also purchased and presented as surprises, no wonder the narcissist seems so perfect at the early phase of a relationship

All the charades of the narcissist are insincere: the "love-bombing" is to get the victim hooked and addicted so that they can proceed to the main reason why they caught the victim, which is to abuse the victim emotionally, to manipulate them mentally, and to use them for their own ends. Love bombing as an endeavour to utilize affection, attention, and warmth to influence someone else; it is a tool of mental manipulation and control; it works on the victim because of a universal need to feel good. We all need to feel good about who we are. This need can't be fulfilled by ourselves, and that is why we seek it in loving relationships with others.

Narcissists are experts at recognizing this need in people, and they are skilled at exploiting it. They detect people with low self-esteem and move to use them. It is possible to identify love bombing right from the start of your relationship with a narcissist and take precautionary measures from the onset because what comes after this stage is something you don't want to experience.

How Do You Protect Yourself from Love-Bombing?

While it is possible at the present moment, you may have someone who is displaying signs of affection towards you, and you can't tell if you are being love-bombed or not. It can often be challenging to differentiate between a person who is naturally kind and affectionate toward you and someone loving with an intent to manipulate.

So how do you know how to protect yourself?

First, it's important to remember that building new relationships into healthy relationships takes time and narcissists in most cases will want to rush the process, so they can get to taking advantage of the victim and achieving their evil intentions.

Also, unlike healthy relationships, in which displays of affection and kindness continue indefinitely, and actions match words, love bombing often involves a sudden change in the type of attention, inconsistent words and actions and an exclusive show of kindness to the person a narcissist desires while being unkind to others.

A right way of protecting yourself from love bombing is to

step back from your new relationship and see it in a different light. Think of your best friend, and the things that you have in common and the things you don't.

Now bring to mind how long it took to build that friendship. Whenever you meet someone and in the space of a few weeks they act like your best friend or seem to know all about you like your best friend, you should beware.

Furthermore, to protect yourself from falling into the trap of love bombing narcissists, beware of anyone who is continually seeking to stroke your ego and push the new relationship to levels you're not ready for. In the early phase of any relationship, don't be scared to slow things down if you feel things are moving too fast at a pace you don't feel comfortable with. Setting boundaries and limiting your contact will keep you from falling for a narcissist, and it will also help you to see your new relationship from a realistic perspective.

Love is naturally healthy and doesn't come in heavy doses of false attention. To avoid being manipulated into an unhealthy relationship at any point, it is crucial for you to keep learning about the ways people seek to manipulate you with your own emotions.

Chapter 2

Devaluation – Honeymoon's Over!

Devaluation is the second cycle of narcissistic abuse in dating; it is the next thing after the narcissist gets bored of love bombing. See, during the love-bombing stage, the victim is treated like "a shiny new object" because the narcissist is obsessed with them.

The victim thinks of love and feels it is being reciprocated while it isn't. The thoughtful acts, unique gifts, "now and forever" promises are to keep the victim at ease and unprepared for what is coming next.

The victim is at ease thinking *"finally, I have found the love of my life"* as love bombing can last for weeks, months, or even more than a year. The victim feels supported, admired, and loved.

There is no time frame for devaluing; you can't for sure say that after ten days, the narcissists take the relationship to this phase. The time frame is different for every narcissist, and it depends on how long they can hold their stuff together and make you believe that you're in an actual loving, fulfilling relationship.

So now you have been completely love bombed or idealized by the narcissist, and you're now completely head-over-heels in love with them, and you believe that they are head-over-heels in love with you too. It is time for them to move on to the next phase.

To a narcissist, a hundred days isn't much time to make the victim think everything is going fine. You will get about a hundred days of love bombing and thinking that everything is so great and so perfect, and also continue thinking that nothing is ever going to change.

Then you get a rude surprise one day.

The relationship hits a painful stage, not physically in most cases, but emotionally because most times, the narcissist doesn't inflict physical pain on the victim but seeks to start wounding, you, the victim, emotionally.

A victim passing through this stage of the cycle might not even know they are being devalued at this point, and that is a sad thing.

Devaluation starts with a drastic shift in the way the narcissist treats the victim, a person who would call and text every day is no longer doing the same. If you had the flu or a cold during the love-bombing phase, this same person would be there for you as a nurse. They might even grab prescriptions for you and take outstanding care of you on the way to recovery.

Devaluation happens pretty cut-and-dry when they start not valuing the way that you feel, what you say, and your actions. The narcissist guilt trips you for doing something that is of value to you or something you were supposed to do as an emphatic human being. A good example is staying late at work to meet an important deadline or attending to a sick grandparent. In cases like this, the narcissist will guilt trip you because of their own constant need for attention.

The lack of responsibility and empathy and constant projection of blame onto others is a characteristic of the narcissist unknown to the victim at the love-bombing phase, and the qualities unknown to the victim come into light gradually at the devaluation phase when the victim has placed their emotional wellbeing in the hands of the narcissist.

Devaluation starts when the narcissist is sure that they have control of the emotional wellbeing of the victim in their hands, and the victim is all hooked in the relationship.

It is effortless for narcissists to find faults in others, even for no good reason. For example, if you wash a car for a narcissist, instead of being grateful for the act, the narcissist will find a fault about the way you washed it or how you didn't clean up a tiny spec of dust on the windscreen. There is no way they are going to appreciate the effort you put into getting their car cleaned.

In romantic relationships at this stage, the partner of the narcissist is trying their best to make them happy and keep them pleased with the relationship, but no matter what they do, it is never enough in the eyes of the narcissist. What makes this stage confusing to the victim is that maybe at times, the narcissist is happy and an absolute delight to be with.

Unknown to the victim in the relationship, the narcissist is only happy when they are trying to get a particular thing they want, and the delightful appearance is to get what they want.

The Devaluing Actions of the Narcissist

- *Verbal*

Verbal devaluing is the words the narcissists say to you as their victim to confuse, strip you of self-identity, make you doubt your sanity and in the end leave you dependent on them for your sense of self-identity.

There are many ways in which the narcissist can use words to devalue you. These are: verbal insults, gaslighting, demanding information or withholding information, threats, projecting blame, and accusations.

Verbal devaluation arises as a result of "weaknesses" in the victim, and the narcissists exploit these weaknesses in entirely different ways.

A good example of verbal devaluation in an intimate relationship is:

"You've got the body of a goddess." (Idealization)

"I think you would look much younger if you work out." (Devaluation)

- *Physical*

Devaluation also comes in actions like being unavailable for you in times of need and distress, or having sex with you despite having STDs and not saying a word about it.

The physical kind of devaluation shows itself readily in many actions of the narcissist. They start to distance themselves away from you and make excuses only to come back abruptly to tell you they are sorry and repeat the cycle over again. When they are confronted, they justify their actions and sweep them under the rug.

- ***Trauma Bonding***

Devaluation also happens through trauma bonding. Trauma bonding is a phenomenon that explains the feelings of love captives have for their captors.

The narcissists can achieve devaluation through trauma bonding because, during the love-bombing phase, they have successfully noted the insecurities of the victim, and know precisely what to say or do to make the victim feel better.

For a victim with self-image issues, the narcissist knows how to provide temporary relief to make the victim more and more dependent. It might even be a childhood wound which the victim is unconscious of that the narcissist keys into.

Why Do Narcissists Seek to Devalue You?

Often, narcissists are delusional and are disconnected from themselves, as outer focused beings, they are toxic, and they don't even connect to themselves in a self-loving and self-supportive way.

So when they are feeling anxious, they will not admit this to anyone else, and since the narcissist can't connect to anyone else on a stable emotional level, they resort to verbal abuse.

Their grandiose sense of delusion also makes them believe that they are the better ones in the relationship. They are always looking for ways to feed their ego, and since they can't lovingly talk to themselves, they look outward for an ego stroke.

Their messed up psyche needs their partners to meet their unrealistic expectations, and also it needs their partner to submit to them alone, and once they discover that they can't get whatever it is they crave, they lash out and feel angry. They punish people for the inner rage they feel for relief.

If anything goes wrong in the narcissist's life, it is not their fault in any way, and when they commit atrocities too, it is not their fault: they are unconscious to what the truth of the matter is, and that is why they seek external sources to lash out on and take responsibility for their misdeeds.

Is it Something You Have Said or Done?

At times, during this stage of the relationship, you start to wonder if you are the problem or not. That is precisely how the narcissist wants you to feel. They gaslight you into thinking you are the issue.

If you are spending time with a partner who is a liar and has no empathy, you will be violated, and you start to behave like an emotionally wounded person.

You may also be confused by what is happening and think

you are the one to blame for the actions of the narcissist.

Being devalued by a narcissist doesn't come in anger bursts and constant criticism alone. It can also present itself as having no concern for you, your activities, or your needs. It may come with objectifying you and treating you like a cheap object. It may also be lying and saying things behind your back that would hurt you.

Devaluation as a stage in the narcissistic abuse cycle features constant accusations and criticisms, gaslighting, lying and cheating, and verbal abuse. If you are in this stage, it is advisable to react calmly or walk away from the relationship so that you don't get stuck in a narcissistic web of manipulation.

It is necessary to state at this point that devaluation doesn't only happen between a narcissist and their victim in a romantic relationship, it also occurs in other relationships of the narcissists because they, the narcissist ,always make people dependent on them and create a situation of co-dependency.

A codependent person relies on an external source for a sense of identity, validation, and approval. Co-dependency makes it easy for the narcissist to manipulate their victims as they prey on this weakness. The victim is dependent on the narcissist for self-love, self-worth, and self-approval.

You are not responsible for the feelings of the narcissist, and you can always find a good relationship with a loving adult who is honest, decent and kind and who isn't still seeking to blame people for how they feel but has accepted the responsibility of how they think like responsible adults.

Finally, devaluing will lead to the narcissist's full discard, which is the next phase that will be expanded upon in the coming chapter.

Chapter 3

Discarding – Run Away and Never Look Back

Having talked about love bombing and devaluing, the next cycle and the final cycle is the discarding stage, and discarding might come temporarily or permanently. Momentarily, they withdraw totally from the victim for only a short while, and definitively, they never speak to the victim again.

Narcissists want attention always, and they will take it, whether it is good or bad. They prefer good, but they will take bad if they can't get the right kind. A narcissist is a person who loves drama and while they are craving any attention from you, they are also ready to dump you and move on to someone else, especially when they have somebody else they can slink right onto.

A temporary discard will have the narcissists coming back to say *"sorry"* and a permanent discard is when they quit talking to you altogether. It depends on the kind of person you are dealing with.

Depending on the kind of narcissist you are dealing with, they might want to discard you publicly or privately. Without any closure, they walk away, and you are getting no single answer for the millions of questions that are going to run through your mind at that point.

In the previous chapter, it was mentioned that there is no specific time frame for the stages a relationship goes through with a narcissist, but this stage shouldn't come as a surprise since the narcissist doesn't come to this phase directly. They love bomb the victim, then move on to devalue them and finally discard them.

It is quite natural for the narcissist to walk away at this point of the relationship, one, because they have found a new narcissistic supply source, and two because they always have little or no emotional investment in a relationship.

Devaluing actions are signs that something is going to happen sooner or later in the relationship, and the lying, cheating, plan canceling, lack of physical intimacy, gaslighting and other symptoms will eventually snowball to one significant point where the relationship ends abruptly.

However, for the narcissist, they can't wait to get to the discarding phase and move on to the next thing; the narcissist is tired of the games, and they want something new.

Perhaps, you are no longer fulfilling a particular function to the narcissist; then it's time for them to cast you aside and abandon you, with no sad parting, no healthy communication.

Discarding you is the last part of the cycle. However, it doesn't mean the death of your relationship with the narcissist as you might be abandoned only temporarily. The reason why a narcissist will seek to drop you only temporarily is that they know how insecure you are and how leaving you might open up a past psychological wound.

Temporarily discarding you will give the narcissist a feeling of great satisfaction knowing they have hurt you emotionally, and they feel important knowing they have such an effect on you. They think they are significant and hold it in their heads that the world revolves around them.

They get a temporary "high" and when they know you are trying to reach them, or you are stalking them after they have discarded you, the "high" feeling hits them again. They will feel happy at hearing about how to hurt you are or how much you miss them.

The signs the narcissist is planning to discard you

The narcissist discards you when they see you are no longer useful to them, they have love-bombed you, and you gave in so that they can devalue you and since they have gotten the "thrill" they sought out to find in the first place, your time is up. Also, the narcissist must have secured another source of narcissistic supply before they make a conscious choice to discard you.

The attention you have given them is no longer good enough for them and its time to move on to a higher quality narcissistic supply.

1. *They are searching for someone new*

The narcissist has begun the hunt for other prey, and you might be aware of this because your gut is telling you they are currently looking for another to replace you.

You observe them on the phone making long calls to a "friend" or "business partner" or "work colleague" and long hours on their social media account and they are now secretive about their emails, phone messages, and social media accounts.

You will also notice a sudden change in their routines and frequent unexplainable unavailability. They might disappear for days without explanation or any contact or tell you long stories and countless lies explaining their behavior.

They might even gaslight you to make you think you are the cause of their change in behavior. You all of a sudden find things where you didn't put them; you might find objects around and you can't explain how they got there.

Evidently, they are trying to gaslight you to think you are the cause of their behavior.

Another pointer at this point are new manners: at this point, they are trying to love to bomb their latest victim, and as such, they are changing their appearance, they are wearing new clothes, they are looking suitable for their potential victim.

You might even notice "triangulation" where you are frequently being compared to someone else; you are being compared to someone you don't know.

2. *The "mask" drops completely*

You have never seen them behave in this way before.

Prior this time, they have been operating under the mask of a healthy person, and now, they have decided to put off the cover because they don't intend to keep you any longer.

They no longer have to keep up with the charade, and there is no need to put on the mask again. You now get to see them for who they are.

Now their full features are amplified and they don't need to keep up with who they once were because it is time to let you go. They don't have any more reasons to reply to your texts as soon as possible, and there is no need to disclose anything important to you again at this point.

At this stage, they don't care about how you feel, and you would observe their inconsistencies and see through their lies. The mask has dropped for you, and they are only putting it on around the new victim.

These signs point to the fact that whatever it is you had with the narcissist wasn't real even though you might desperately want it to be real. You might feel or be sick, and this is due to the cognitive dissonance you feel at this point.

The narcissists discard you just because they have found other sources of narcissistic supply and they might come back in the future to use you as a tool to punish whoever their current partner is.

Know that the three cycles of narcissistic manipulation go hand in hand, and you might be recruited again for the narcissist's agenda. For the sake of your sanity and your well being, rereadthe information about these stages and see if they don't apply to you or someone you know.

Having established the cycles of narcissistic abuse, it is time to move on to the types of narcissists and the tactics they use to seduce their victims and the ones they use in manipulating and abusing their partners in relationships.

In the next section, we will examine some of the different tactics narcissists employ in their manipulation game and how effective these tactics are for them. The tactics discussed in the subsequent section are the most common tactics used by narcissists, and that is the reason why they are featured.

Narcissistic Manipulation In Dating

Chapter 4

The Overt Narcissist and The Covert Narcissist

There exists a particular distinction between the type of narcissists in psychology: overt narcissists, and covert narcissists. This classification is based on the personalities of the two kinds of narcissists and the behavior they exhibit dominantly. The significant difference between the two types of narcissists will be expanded on in this chapter.

The two different kinds of narcissist operate differently in intimate relationships, and they also explore the tactics that will be discussed later on in different ways, but one thing is common to the two kinds of the narcissist, and that is that they seek to manipulate others, including their partners, to do their bidding.

The Overt Narcissist.

"Blimey! Is that the time? I haven't even gotten to the part where 'I' had to save the day. She messed it all up. It was left to 'me' to save the day. If 'I' had not been there, they would not have survived without 'me.'"

Ever been in a social gathering of friends or colleagues and there is that one person who keeps on talking about himself/herself only to find their words a perambulation of self-eulogy?

Overt narcissists are narcissists with an extroverted nature.

An overt narcissist is someone who openly, without any reservation, cares about himself and nothing else. This is the type of person who tends to be loud, arrogant, self-absorbed, insensitive, and puts him/herself under the spotlight. This person feeds off the attention of others. As fish is to water, so is an overt narcissist to being in the spotlight looking for compliments.

How do they behave?

This is perhaps the most accessible type of narcissist to identify. Individuals who fall into this category are outward with this personality trait. There is no ambiguity when it comes to them except when they are manipulative.

Overt narcissists walk into a room and immediately look for ways to become the center of attention. They cannot stand other people being in the spotlight. They, in some way or capability, have to show themselves as though performing in front of an audience. They tend to look down on their peers while they surround themselves with those, who by being in their vicinity, elevate their status and prestige.

Overt narcissists are the ones you find being heartless towards others. They strive for success and happiness even at the expense of others.

Their unique traits include but are not restricted to:

1. Arrogance.
2. Attention demanding.
3. Mocking and degrading others.
4. Viewing people as stepping stones.
5. Being prone to outbursts when not satisfied.
6. Manipulative
7. Defensive and combative
8. Looking for opportunities to outshine and outclass others publicly.

How do they choose to manipulate victims?

In the case of an overt narcissist, he/she tends to suppress others in a bid to feel empowered. Two reasons why they would "hang" out with you are that you have something they want, and by getting it, it boosts their ego and that you have nothing to offer but your presence reminds them of how better off they are.

How the overt narcissist operates in an intimate relationship; How they treat their boyfriends/girlfriends

This is a tricky subject for a lot of people because many are in denial that they are in mentally, physically, or emotionally abusive relationships. It starts with their choice. Overt narcissists tend to either be in a relationship where the partner is physically alluring or emotionally weak.

For those who go into a relationship with physically alluring partners, they do so for the attention. A narcissistic man/woman who goes into a relationship with a physically alluring partner feeds off of the attention their partner gets, which invariably makes them look good. Questions like, "how did you get him/her to fall in love with you?", "What's your secret?" Have a way of fueling the egos of narcissists. They primarily tend to go for such people (physically appealing) specifically for such moments. It is like being in high school all over again. The hottest girl ending up with the hottest guy, the only difference being, one of them is only in the relationship for the attention it brings and not necessarily for the commitment.

On the other hand, overt narcissists in relationships with emotionally weak individuals enjoy the power of being in charge. It feeds their ego to astronomical heights. Emotionally fragile individuals tend to be dependent on their partners, and by doing so, they invariably cause their narcissistic partners to feel like gods in their relationship. They are in constant supply of their needed attention in such a relationship.

Remember, a narcissistic individual is all about himself and craves attention, which is why an overt narcissist does this without any conscience.

Examples of how overt narcissists treat their partners.

1. Overt narcissists tend to be self-appointed know it alls.

The opinions, thoughts or contribution of their girlfriend or boyfriend tends to be corrected, marginalized or sometimes invalidated and this can be embarrassing especially when it is done in public gatherings such as parties, meetings, and the likes.

You might once have noticed that the conversation might have started with you but all of a sudden, thirty minutes into the conversation and it is no longer about you but about himself/herself. He/she might be the type to listen to you and nod along with what you are saying only to interrupt you later and revert the conversation to himself/herself or back to what they were speaking on earlier.

2. Controlling.

They can be controlling, not giving you enough space to fully express yourself, which is as a result of insecurity and no longer being the center of your attention. Therefore, they fuel their ego to feel relevant. They also present themselves as saviors as it puts them in a position of superiority.

3. Manipulative.

Such a person is not concerned about your emotions, unless they somehow serve his/her cause. He/she might coerce or repeatedly insist on having their way by warming up to you to get their way. Doing this further nourishes their ego. They can play the victim, be upset, or bring up old hurts caused by you to guilt-trip and hurt you in return.

4. Difficult

Overt narcissists can deliberately be difficult, and this is because watching their boyfriend or girlfriend get flustered gives them a sense of importance. They do this simply because they can, and it gets them the needed reaction.

They can choose to disagree with you purely because it is 'fun.' Your reaction makes them matter as opposed to nothing. A response, to them, is the needed validation that they still matter.

The Covert Narcissist

A covert narcissist is someone who has almost the same characteristics as the covert narcissist, but goes about it in an entirely different way but achieves the same result.

Covert narcissists are naturally introverts in nature as opposed to overt narcissists. They tend to be more subtle in their relations with others, but the result is always the same.

How do they behave?

It is easier to spot overt narcissism than covert narcissism as the latter is not straightforward. Often it isn't until the victim has fallen into the trap that they realize, albeit late, that they have had their emotions played with.

Consider a hamburger. You can order a large, small or medium-sized burger but the fact is it is still a hamburger. That is the same principle here. Covert narcissism can be considered the small burger.

They tend to be more reclusive, but it is not necessarily true. Covert narcissists take their time to study their surroundings and people to find and exploit individuals who they deem as prey. They can portray themselves as timid, but it is a ploy to garner attention. They are not particular about the attention of the masses but are content with the few they have. They are manipulative, and emotions are their means of getting what they want. They have a higher thirst for attention than overt narcissists as they are slightly weaker emotionally.

Their unique features.

1. Toys with emotions and attentions and utilizes them as a tool.
2. Self-pity is an arsenal.
3. He/she paints himself/herself as a victim.
4. Exaggerates on stories that will garner pity and concern.
5. He/she sees himself/herself as a victim of abuse, trauma, or depression.
6. He/she blames others.
7. He/she creates commotion to gain attention.
8. Sees life as unfair and thinks he/she is being treated poorly by others.

How does the covert narcissist choose to manipulate victims?

Covert narcissists do not go to the extremes overt narcissists do to gather attention; they are not seen at the forefront of the limelight but rather at the back. They play the victim, or a disturbed or hurt individual, and this works as people tend to sympathize and develop an urge to help.

They intentionally place themselves in a compromising situation just to be rescued or helped. They tend to be emotionally weak and exploit other emotionally vulnerable individuals.

How the covert narcissist operates in an intimate relationship; how they treat their boyfriends/girlfriends

In relationships, covert narcissists could be said to be more formidable than overt narcissists when considering the emotional rollercoaster they put their victims through. A covert narcissist never seems to run out of excuses in a relationship.

They can be clingy and quick to be jealous. Narcissists love the attention that they get from being the 'only' one. Irrespective of the sacrifices made by their partners, a covert narcissist rarely gets satisfied. Every new day becomes another opportunity to demand attention.

They tend to become dependent on their partners, and this is not as a result of a COVERT narcissist being incapable of taking care of himself/herself, but such dependency gives them the level of intimacy and attention they need and want.

They lack empathy towards their partner's needs and are solely focused on theirs. An example of this could be going out for dinner. He/she might want to dine at an expensive restaurant, but you might not have the money for it. Rather than understand your present limitations, he/she would probably fake tears, become moody, act out, or ruin the rest of your evening.

Another good example is you could have had a bad day and be stressed out at work and try to communicate that to your partner only to have them complain about you not having time for them or not sacrificing as much as he/she does in the relationship. Covert narcissists tend to whip out the 'guilt trip' card any time.

In such relationships, their partners tend to find that they are becoming increasingly fatigued emotionally, mentally, and physically as covert narcissists can be draining to their partners.

They are not willing to be called out on their wrongs and would instead blame it on their partners or blame it on a past incidence. It is never them to be blamed. In extreme cases, they would flip it around and give reasons why they are the victim of what you claim they did, which was ultimately as a result of your earlier actions leading to the present moment. (Do you follow?)

Creating confusion in relationships is another tactic of a covert narcissist. What this accomplishes is a confused partner who starts to doubt themselves, making them further subjectable to manipulation. Doing this gives them leverage and gives them power over their partners.

They have a way of making it seem like you are the one with the problem. They can disregard you in crucial moments such as canceling a date last minute, ignoring your calls, being online and chatting with others but not replying to your messages, or giving a definite answer. Remember, covert narcissists prey on the emotionally weak and as such their partners are no different thereby lacking the necessary willpower to walk away from an abusive relationship causing them to invariably become dependent on their partners despite being treated this way. Their partners do not seem to have enough courage to walk away, making them susceptible to further manipulation.

It takes a great deal of effort to receive compliments from a covert narcissist. Compliments elevate you, and that is something they cannot afford. They need to be in control always. Whatever they do, all that matters is how they feel and the attention they get. That is why they cannot afford to be seen publicly in a negative light. Hence, they treat their partners better in public than they do when no one is around as it gives the needed attention they want so badly.

Although it can be said that at the end of the day a narcissist is a self-absorbed individual who craves attention, the two categories, overt narcissist and covert narcissist, consist of different individuals who achieve the same result through various methods.

Where a covert narcissist could be seen as someone who is subtle in his behavior, an overt narcissist is the complete opposite. Overt narcissists can be loud and direct about their approach, often being blunt and straightforward whereas a covert would be more diplomatic, dropping subtle hints that elude to those they interact with. They still produce the same result though.

Chapter 5

The Narcissist's Harem

What exactly is a narcissist's harem, and how does it count as a manipulation tactic when a narcissist finds a new victim? This might be a few of many questions that come to mind at the sight of this chapter's title. To grasp the concept of a narcissist's harem, let's continue with an untold part of Nicole and Jones' story.

When Nicole and Jones started dating for a couple of weeks, Jones had explained to her that he has a lot of female friends, but she never saw it as a threat to their relationship until she discovered later on that over seventy-five per cent of his friends on Facebook and two-thirds of his phone contacts were women.

She began to have the feeling of been investigated by those ladies as they would not stop sending her friend requests on Facebook, looking to penetrate her affairs to unravel her dirt.

At first, she thought the feeling of been investigated was because of competition between her and other ladies. Jones was a charming man and the dream of every lady.

What Nicole didn't know is that she was the new prey the lion was sharing his attention with because she was the fresh catch and was still sparkly, and every other lady was relegated to the end of the line.

The Narcissist Harem are the people a narcissist goes back to when they need care. These can include friends and family members, but fundamentally they are people they used to date, their former boyfriends or girlfriends, people that gave them attention previously, people who at a time did not give them the privileges they wanted or new people they seek to pull into their web.

When a narcissist is with a member of their Narcissist Harem, they exhibit an inflated sense of importance, a deep need for excessive attention and admiration, a lack of empathy, and often a lot of conflict.

Examples of Narcissist Harem Roles

Shiny objects move narcissists as they are fickle creatures and they often replace the objects as swiftly as they have obtained them, they are used to manufacturing love triangles to make their partners jealous and compete for their attention and approval.

In the eyes of the narcissist, every harem is replaceable and interchangeable depending on what they can offer to the narcissist.

Contrary to popular belief, the role of a Narcissist Harem can be changed at any time, and this is as a result of what the narcissist perceives. There are five examples of Narcissist Harem roles:

1. The Love-Bombed Target

This is when a potential Narcissist Harem member just becomes the girlfriend or boyfriend of the Narcissist, and he/she has been treated like a king or queen, and the Narcissist presents the new potential member of the Narcissist Harem as the best.

The new target is considered infallible by the narcissist, so the narcissist gives all attention to the victim at the detriment of others and showers excessive praise, special favor, and flattery on the victim.

This care makes the new object of affection become the subject of jealousy from the other victims who once occupied the position of the Harem, but within a short time, the victim is also relegated.

2. The Ride-or Die-Enablers

The most devoted of the Narcissist Harem is the 'ride-or-die' enablers for the narcissist. They must shield the narcissist from accountability and defend the excessive entitled attitude of the narcissist towards things they desire.

They can do anything immoral to save the head of the narcissist and shut down any complaints from anyone who dares to question the behavior of the narcissist. They also act as shields and bullies, and taunt any target threatening to come at the narcissist. They are devoted followers of the narcissist who can perpetrate various schemes, whether immoral or unjust because of the narcissist. Examples of such are parents, siblings, colleagues at work, friends, or anyone who has become a devout follower of the narcissist.

3. The Right-Hand-Man or Woman

This is an individual who assists the narcissist in breaking laws and order, and who has aligned to the values of the narcissist. A victim of the narcissist will not fill into this role at all. This person is irreplaceable to the narcissist as they are self-centered, not empathic, and exploitative in their view. Hence they are always with the narcissist for a long time. They are usually the best friend, confidant, and partner of the narcissist but just like others they can be replaced once the narcissist gets a better and new option.

4. The Empathic-Caretakers

The individual usually fills this role with the most compassionate and empathic yet blinded perso. This is a person often bonded by trauma to the narcissist and Harem. This set of people feel the narcissist is the right individual who cares for them and wants the best for them.

The narcissist often does not need good people, but they surround themselves with people who care so much as this empathic person is only used to draw other people into the net of the narcissist. These caregivers often portray the right image for the narcissist as a generous person, and this gives a 'social proof' that the narcissist has the support of people who are morally different from them.

5. The Scapegoat

This individual is the punching bag of the narcissist and every other member of the Narcissist Harem. They are often treated with disdain and blamed for whatever bad things happen to the narcissist. They are often ignored by the narcissist whenever other members of the Harem are praised.

How do you know someone who is in a Narcissist Harem and how Narcissist Operate them

Imagine the feeling of been humiliated, mercilessly manipulated, and ridiculed. Your personality has been eroded and diminished as you see yourself as a misfit. Perhaps you have gone through the cycle of abuse several times within a short time. Maybe you have been harassed, lied to, and bullied to stick to your abuser. This is precisely what it means to be in a Narcissist Harem as the narcissist engages in verbal and emotional abuse towards their victims. If you see yourself experiencing any of the signs below, it is an indication that you are in a Narcissist Harem.

1. Experiencing dissociation just to survive

This is the feeling of emotional and physical detachment from society, and experiencing disruptions in your memory, perceptions, and sense of self. Separation is, of course, the essence of trauma, and it does result in emotional deadening in the face of terrible situations. The victim finds ways to block the impact of the pains experienced emotionally, so he/she does not deal with the total danger of the circumstance.

2. Walking on Eggshells

The Harem begins to avoid places, people, or activities that can provide relief. The trauma caused by narcissism might result in the victim not picking up phone calls from family members and not attending social functions. This, however, does not help the victim as the narcissist still abuses the victim anytime the narcissist chooses to use the victim as a punching bag.

3. Putting aside your needs and sacrificing everything only to please the abuser

Since the life of the Narcissist Harem revolves around the narcissist, the goals, hobbies, and friendships of the victim have all been sacrificed just to make the abuser happy in the relationship. The victim, however, has to do more to please the narcissist who actually never gets satisfied.

4. Battling with health issues and somatic symptoms that represent your psychological turmoil

The stress caused by abuse from a narcissist may send the cortisol levels of the victim into overdrive and result in the suppression of the immune system, leaving the victim vulnerable to illnesses and diseases. Sleeping also becomes difficult as the mind flashbacks to the painful experiences caused by the abuse.

5. Developing no trust

Everyone appears to be a threat, and there is so much anxiety about what others can do, especially after having been battered by someone the victim trusted. There is, therefore, a hard time trusting anyone, including yourself.

6. Having suicidal thoughts or self-harming tendencies

Depression and anxiety usually result in a sense of hopelessness as the circumstance becomes unbearable as if there is no way out. Thoughts of harming yourself by taking poison or jumping from a cliff do frequent the mind of the victim.

7. Comparing yourself to others, and blaming yourself for the abuse

Due to the multiple people in the triangle of the narcissist, the victim begins to compete for the attention of the abuser for care and approval. The victim starts to ask "why me" and blame him or herself for the abuse instead of the abuser.

8. Self-sabotage and self-destruction

The victim meditates on the abuse and hears the voice of the abuser in his mind, thereby increasing negative self-talk and possibility of self-sabotage, and this often results in suicide.

9. Fear of doing what you love doing and achieving success

The sense of worthlessness pushes the victim to never believing in himself; this conditions the mind of the victim to failure and hopelessness.

To bring an end to this chapter, it should be stated again that a Narcissist Harem is a group of people the narcissist goes back to when they need care, and these people are not limited to just family and friends, but also previous partners, and whoever gave them attention in the past.

Chapter 6
They will HOOVER you!

WHAT IS HOOVERING?

Imagine an ex who abused you sexually, talked you down and beat you several times, reaching out to you after a breakup and trying to be your friend again. This is someone who never valued you while you dated and he wants to renew the friendship just because he needs what he is not getting from you.

Or,

Imagine an ex who abused you verbally, and played with your emotions, reaching out to you long after the break up trying to be your friend again. This is a woman who never valued you while the whole relationship lasted.

Hoovering is an attitudinal pattern connected with narcissistic personality disorder (NPD).

Narcissists make contact with one or any of their former lovers after a period of separation when they discover they have moved on with their life. Hoovering happens when the narcissist seeks to suck their victim back into the relationship after the Narcissist, and their partner has not communicated in a long time, and the insincerity of the narcissist characterizes it.

Hoovering is an emotional abuse technique used by the narcissists to get the victim back into their sphere by using several manipulative personality types with the victim. It often happens when the narcissist is running low on supply, and they need to suck their victims back into the relationship with them. Hoovering is basically like treating a partner like dirt.

A narcissist perception of their victim is that they are prey, servicing their pleasure anytime they are hungry. A narcissist will always want to be in charge so whenever they have lost control of their victim, they come back to prove they are superior to the victim by using various tactics of narcissistic abuse.

The narcissist believes whatever belongs to them can never be taken away from them, so they ensure to suck back the victim into a relationship. The narcissist derives pleasure from harming the victims as a lion kills his prey, ensuring victims are never happy, and they are hopeless about life.

This kind of abuse consists of intentional acts of hurting to the extent that it results in symptoms similar to PTSD or Stockholm syndrome and a disorder. The narcissist has an addiction to making their victims miserable always, and the narcissist does relieve themselves with alcohol, cigarettes, and other hard drugs.

A male narcissist is an exploiter, and he intentionally hoovers to test a vaccine, mercilessly opening the wounds of his victim to enable him to suck the supply.

The victim is needed when there is a significant need like sex, money, or attention, and the narcissist only returns when he is short of what the victim is capable of supplying. After the narcissist gets supply from his victim, he throws a party. His words of love are not sincere as he only says it for love-bombing, a technique employed as part of a bigger plan to neutralize and bait the victim and gain their trust. Whenever the narcissist love-bombs he sweeps his victim off their feet with a motive to exploit the victim. This love-bomb is so that he can get his next fix.

A narcissist abuses his victims mercilessly with no remorse, and he seeks to inflict wounds and violate the rights of his victims. He proves to be superior with how he bullies his victims, recaptures them, manipulates and subverts the mind and will of his ex. He does this by tearing down every sense of worth, value and self of his victim and instills in his victim anxiety, terror, doubt and confusion. All these contribute to the victim dissociating from people, talking to his or herself and getting depressed.

A narcissist believes in entitlement forever, and he wants to suck out supply from his victim forever, so he is always on the lookout to maintain a double standard in terms of entitlement. The narcissist is domineering, so he feels entitled to get and keep all the fun and ecstasies of the relationship. They do this by erecting themselves as small gods to their victims and tear down every sense of self of their victim.

Hoovering occurs when a narcissist returns to ensure his past partner is trapped on an emotional roller coaster, deceived by falsehoods and deceptions. He is ruthless and callous towards his victim's pains and renders his victim powerless. His desire always is to be hated, and he is glad when his victim begins to act violently towards him and also hates him. He is excited how his partner feels after feeling bad for hating him as he knows this makes her feel miserable.

The same is true for the female narcissist, too; she hoovers her victim because she believes the world revolves around her, and she can get whatever she wants whenever she wants it.

HOW A NARCISSIST ATTEMPTS TO HOOVER THEIR VICTIMS IN DATING

To avoid being sucked in by the hoovering tricks of a narcissist, it is expedient to know how they operate in relationships; they can go to any length to get you back in their circle and suck you like a vacuum sucks up dirt in your carpet. Falling into their tricks makes them satisfied as it is all about them and not about you and they only came back to see their level of influence on you and the moment they discover they are still in control, they get back to abusing you.

You need to be careful not to fall into the schemes of narcissists, and the following are the attempts narcissists engage in when hoovering their victims in relationships.

1. Act like there was no breakup

Narcissists will always act like there was no break up by trying to be careful if it has been a long time since they have communicated with you. They know you have moved on with life, but after some months, they send you a romantic text telling you of the date you first had with them. The first night you had sex with them and shortly after reading the text message, you hear a knock on the door, and it is a dispatch rider with a parcel containing rose flowers from the narcissist. What a blossoming sentiment, you suddenly pick up your phone to retrieve their number to call them asking for lunch and thank them for the text message and the rose flowers. You are already sucked back.

2. I love you, I adore you, and I can never do without you

Everyone desires to be shown love and to be cared for, and no one wants to resist love as it invokes feelings of happiness and value. It communicates the feeling of being understood and someone wanting to spend time with you. Narcissists understand desire as a need for every human being, and they use the "love" and "adore" as a tool to get you back into their trap. Their kind of love is a love on a mission to suck supply out of their victims and get what they need urgently and then move on.

3. The important and Romantic Hoover

A narcissist is aware of the sweet moment you had together, so he leverages on your memories of what happened when you were with him and feeds your emotions on these events.

He sends a message of reminiscence and reminds you of every romantic moment and also tells you how you have always appeared in their dreams in their arms.

4. The "Accidental" communication

This happens in two ways: the narcissists sends a text or calls and asks if the victim called or he planned to send the text to someone else. Any of these tricks is an avenue to lure the victim back into his domain and start a conversation. If the victim responds to the text or returns the call, it is an opportunity for the narcissist to suck supply from the victim and within a short time, you are servicing his needs consistently and going through the cycle of abuse.

5. There is trouble

It can be emotional hearing someone you love is going through turbulent times, as ruthless as the person might be since you have always shared something in common and you want to be with them. The narcissist takes advantage of this moment to lure the victim over by, for example, telling the victim there is nobody to care for his needs as everyone has deserted him for one reason or the other. The victim gets emotional and probably moves into the house of the narcissist to care and comfort them in every possible way even if it is against their norms. The truth is the crisis was either exaggerated or never existed.

6. Getting someone to test the waters

The narcissist is smart but acts like a coward by sending someone whom you cherish and respect to contact you as they don't want their ego bruised by a face-to-face rejection. The narcissist gets feedback from the person he sends to you and takes advantage of this to make you cave in.

7. Apologizing repeatedly

The narcissist assures the victim they will never be foolish again and repeatedly apologizes for every mistake, but the change is just for a moment as he cannot change. The apology is not a genuine one as they only want to appeal to your emotions and suck you till you are empty and worthless.

Narcissists are players and can talk to suck you in and keep you in their fold. It is expedient you know they only care about what they will get from you and not about you.

Chapter 7
The Gaslighting Trick

Gaslighting is a kind of abuse where a partner attempts to get his/her partner to believe he/she is "crazy" as a way of dominating him/her. The word "gaslighting" originated from a 1938 play, "Gaslight", in which a husband begins to gradually make his wife crazy by making the gaslight in the house dim at random times and denying anything ever happened. His wife begins to doubt her own experiences, and shortly, she doesn't know what to believe again.

Gaslighting is an abusive tactic that takes the form of either environmental verbal or emotional exploitation. Anytime gaslighting is used on anyone, they feel frustrated because they are made to feel their senses are not functioning properly.

Gaslighting often occurs when a narcissist consistently lies to, confuses and misleads their lover about occurrences that have taken place. They usually tell their partner that they didn't hear well or cause a lot of confusion by overreacting. It's a way of gaining control and power over a partner by the use of lies and deceptions which are very convincing but blatant. The narcissist is so bold and confident that the victim is confused and starts to feel destabilized, confused, and dependent on the narcissist.

This feeling of insecurity and incompetence makes the victim desire to always be around the narcissist all the time. Gaslighting is a method adopted by the narcissist to hide the abuse and lie with a goal, and it takes place in friendships, work, family, government, amongst cult leaders, and advertising commercials.

There are several scenarios of gaslighting. If you still doubt whether you have become a victim of gaslighting, the following examples will convince you on the subject matter.

Relationships: Bridget has been dating Samuel for five years, and she has always wanted to go into the movie industry, but Samuel has always been angry at her.

He says acting in Hollywood would not allow her to spend time with him. She feels her dream of being an actress was creating a rift between her and her boyfriend. She decided to drop the idea because of her boyfriend, but despite all her efforts of saving her relationship, her boyfriend still calls her "crazy" just because she forgot to switch off the bulb in the bathroom.

Family: Frank grew up to know his father to be abusive as often his father tells him he is a nonentity, a complete loser, bastard, and he can never amount to anything. Frank is always unhappy and is surprised when his friends in school talk about their father's love, how they shower gifts on them. One day after school, he confronted his dad, who was drinking alcohol, about why he usually talks him down. His father tells him to stop sleeping and face the reality of life.

Work: Jeff has been a diligent and hardworking employee. He has a new female manager, Brenda, who he liked and he was able to complete every task given to him by her every day. After a while, his manager begins to send him demeaning errands, and though Jeff continues to help his boss with these errands, his boss continues to demand more.

She begins to question the capability of Jeff, telling him to focus on his primary duty at work. Brenda appraised Jeff and scored him low. Jeff approached her and asked why she scored him low in the appraisal; she says he was quite sluggish and could not work unless he was supervised. Jeff resolved to accept to do all the chores she sends him no matter how much work it caused and belittling it was.

HOW NARCISSISTS USE GASLIGHTING ON THE PEOPLE THEY DATE

If you ever feel a narcissist gaslights you, then you currently have negative emotions, and you feel anxious and depressed every time as you blame yourself for every event that takes place. Gaslighting often occurs alongside other kinds of abuse, for example financial, domestic violence or sexual abuse.

Gaslighting can be so insidious, that you don't even realize it is happening in your relationship, and while you might be confused about what to trust, know it is as a result of the seeds of doubt already sown in your mind.

The techniques narcissists use to gaslight the people they date may include the following:

1. Changing the topic of the conversation

When a narcissist discovers you have a point to make in any communication, and he does not want you to know you have a valid point, he quickly changes the topic suddenly. He does this by diverting the course of the conversation by asking another question or making a proclamation usually aimed at your thoughts. For instance, you are in the car with your toxic partner and two other people are also in the car with you and you guys are driving to a particular place. When you feel he is missing the direction to the area and you tell him politely "You seem to be missing the route to our destination" you will get "No, you are wrong, do you even know how to drive?" or "Did your dad ever have the opportunity to drive a car at all?". The response makes you feel terrible.

2. Discrediting you

Narcissists will discredit their victims by choosing never to believe what they say and making them feel whatever they say is irrational. For example, you tell your partner about how you were celebrated at work for an excellent job you did and how you have been recommended for an increase in salary and promotion. And then the response you get from him is "I believe you are getting the promotion and raise because your boss has feelings for you and he considers showering you with an increase in salary and promotion is an excellent way to win you over as I do not see anything exceptional about you."

3. Wearing a mask of confidence forcefulness/fake

compassion

A narcissist makes you feel you are never right and that you can never achieve anything as a person, so you begin to doubt your abilities and instead believe the stories of your past which the narcissist is fully aware of. You will think the narcissist is actually compassionate about you and wants the best for you by always letting you know you are never right and that every decision you have ever taken has always ended up to be disastrous.

4. Twisting the facts

After making a statement in which you are sure what you said is the truth and is correct, the narcissist twists and reframes what you said and confuses you, so you doubt whether your statement was true or false. This is actually done to favor them and demean you as you begin to have the feeling of incompetence even in things you are an expert at doing as they intend to make you feel unstable and irrational. For example, you made a statement about the United States as the highest debtor globally, and he says it can never be true because the dollar is still robust and the economy of the United States is still booming.

Of course, they know the truth, but they have the motive to confuse you and take you off balance.

5. Minimizing

Your personality is trivialized, and the gaslighter gains more control and authority over you as you become powerless. For example, "You need not pick offense because I said does your dad have a car, I was only joking" or "you take things too seriously".

Can I make it out of this "gaslighting" thing?

Do you feel you are gaslighted? It is not the end of the world, as it does not change the fact that you are depressed or emotionally imbalanced. It's right for you to know that you are not the first person and you would not be the last person that would be gaslighted as several people out there are yet to realise that they are gaslighted by a narcissist.

Ensure you listen to your intuition and if you feel there is something wrong with your relationship and you are being gaslighted, never try to sort everything out on your own. Instead seek help from a professional who will be willing to help you out.

Chapter 8

Future Faking

Referring to a narcissist as a liar is not as important as analyzing the type of lies he tells: Future Faking. This implies that a narcissist talks about a collective future to get what they want immediately. They employ Future Faking as a tool to manage the emotions and expectations of victims.

Let us look at another story here, Ken and Lucy's story:

Ken was a charming guy; he met Lucy at the train station on a Monday morning on his way to work.

They exchanged contacts and, they dated for some couple of months; after that, Ken introduced Lucy to his family members.

Since Lucy had a bigger apartment compared to Ken's apartment, he decided to move into her flat. She pays all the bills in the house, feeds him, buys him clothes and satisfies him sexually almost every time.

Things stopped being a fairy tale as he stopped coming home and started seeing another girl, whom he later moved in with.

In future faking, the victim is promised money tomorrow so there can be money available and telling you there is no money tomorrow when you come requesting for cash.

Future Faking involves overestimating oneself by hyping the future to get what you desire in the present from a partner. It consists of telling your partner what they want to hear to get their attention; there is the tendency for us to act that way as individuals to enjoy the flattery of the reactions of the people we tell lies to.

Often times, the narcissist forgets that they need to deliver on their promises of things happening in the future as they are only particular about the present situation, namely what they can obtain from the victim.

They easily avoid accountability of their promises, evading responsibility and liability is what they do best, and you can never hold them to fulfill their pledges as all you will find is denial, guesses or another charm nasty in which you have retreated on on the basis of additional future faking.

Narcissists test the waters with their offensive charm, and once their victim responds positively to their appeal and condones their attitude with having few boundaries, they see an opportunity for confirmation that the victim is expectant of something real.

Some people never fall victim of the antics of the narcissist whenever they use the future faking to suck supply from them. But a narcisst who has allowed their victim to meet their family members, friends, workers, talks about his emotions, talks about the future and how their wedding will be, how their holiday will be spent and how many babies they will have will be a dangerous person.

People with integrity will never lie to a person just to win them over and suck supply out of them as they are truthful and value integrity.

The narcissist usually breaks every promise periodically, and they follow it up with another sign. The continuous promises broken of course insinuate a promised future, and anytime they are broken, it hurts the victim. The narcissist is in the habit of coming with the kind of future you have in mind, and this is worse than lying to anyone. When the future does not appear favorable, and it is effortless to ignore the lack of honesty and blame oneself.

Examples of Future Faking

1. I am aware we've not been together long, but we should get married.

2. Obviously, I will go and see somebody for some assistance; I want to do the appropriate thing for us.

3. I will compensate you.

4. I will, on no account, hurt you.

5. I will, on no account, hurt you another time.

6. I will buy tickets for that event for the two of us, no problem at all.

7. I can't wait to take you on vacation to somewhere

extraordinary.

8. I will get it across to you next week.

9. I promise I will give you a call you tomorrow.

10. I won't tell anyone about what happened.

11. We both have a great future together.

12. I see us aging together and having great kids.

13. I cannot wait for us to start our family.

14. If we go into business together, it makes sense.

15. I will ensure I help you when you have a new job.

16. We need to make plans to travel around the world in our private jet alone.

17. Let us buy our house, move in and live together.

18. I will always be available anytime you need me.

19. Let's start making wedding plans.

20. I will buy you a brand new car for your birthday gift.

HOW NARCISSISTS USE FUTURE FAKING IN THEIR RELATIONSHIPS

Here are some of the ways that a narcissist will use future-faking to keep the victims in their fold for consistent sucking of supply:

1. Future-faking throughout the love-bombing stage

A narcissist makes his lover feel he wants the same things that she does in life. This is referred to as soulmate effect. Example: "Oh my God, you are a Chelsea fan too! Look, they're playing Barcelona next week at Camp Nou. I'll get two tickets for us, we have a date already!" or "The very first time I saw you at the train station, I just knew we were meant for each other because we bonded so easily."

2. Future-faking as a hoovering method

After the narcissist has got what he wants and has had enough, he stops contacting you. He is aware he can always lure you back with ease anytime with little things he knows excites you. Future-faking is his back-up plan in his bag of hoovering antics. Example "Feel my heartbeat. Can't you see how much I love and admire you? I want to live with you, grow old together, and die together."

3. Future-faking to end a fight

During the middle of a disagreement, the narcissist feels he has lost control; he will immediately throw out some future-fakery to make you give up control. Example: "It's okay, look, let's just stop this nonsense and get married and have kids?"

4. Future-faking as part of the conversation.

Narcissists enjoy being heard during every conversation and consequently will lie about the future just to ensure the conversation keep going. Example: "Hey, I've thought that with your expertise, you can help me start my business. What is your take? Do you see us doing it together?"

Dealing with Future Fakers

You see two people in love, and there is future fakery between them, and so you ask yourself, are they having fun? The truth is it prevents the victim from ever trusting anyone again and makes them feel conned and humiliated.

Being future faked means some people become very pessimistic about relationships and dating. It has helped them become stronger emotionally, intellectually, and given them physical and mental boundaries about who they were and what they wanted. It made them knowledgeable and enlightened, and they were not swept away by a narcissist.

If you're serious about dating a guy for marriage, you must differentiate future faking from sincere intentions. The best way to do this is to avoid future pretending yourself: running for your dear life and disregarding your boundaries, sincere intentions, and desires for instantaneous pleasure. Yes, it might mean fewer guys will be coming to you, but by changing what you're interested in, you're also becoming accessible to people of like minds who desire genuine love and relationships.

Chapter 9

Flying Monkeys

Despite the hurt and frustration the victims of narcissists have to deal with just because they are in love with the narcissist, several of the victims see themselves as stranded and lonely because they have turned everyone away. There are some other folks whose job is to add more insult to the injury, and they are messengers for the narcissists.

These guys are called the "flying monkeys" and their job is to take side with the narcissist and ensure that the victim is damaged totally. They are the wicked associates of the narcissist, and they ensure that the victim of the narcissist is tormented even after breaking communication with the abuser.

The kindness and sympathy of the flying monkeys is what makes them easy for the narcissist to control. They cry a lot and make the victim feel that everything that ever happened was caused by the victim and they have a mission just to win you over because they are aware you don't know their tactics. If they ever convince you and you agree to their gimmicks after thinking you had escaped the tyranny of the narcissist, then it might not be over yet as the flying monkeys will bring destruction into your life and make you miserable.

Flying monkeys are referred to as enablers of the narcissists, and they could be friends, family members, religious leaders, and counselors. It is disheartening knowing that your friend, pastor, or family member is a flying monkey. But this is not a new thing as human beings cannot be trusted, and are only mere mortals.

Narcissists take advantage of the relationship you have with these flying monkeys to manipulate and cast these people against you. Often times the flying monkeys are just doing what they do, and they don't realize it as they actually just believe in fulfilling the dream of the narcissist and making sure they are happy. They act on behalf of the abuser as a third party, for an abusive purpose usually.

You need to be on the alert as reasonable, logical, and sensible friends can be turned into sycophants easily, ready to do whatever the narcissist wants them to do. The reasons why a person might decide to be a flying monkey could be numerous, as they may be made to take a one-sided perspective. Members of their family could be on a mission to help a troublesome relative. The mutually dependent would want to keep enjoying the influence of the narcissist for their own hostile instincts and others may have been influenced by the personality of the narcissist to define the circumstance along the narcissist's personal lines.

John and Mary dated for three years and John often beat Mary in the relationship and cheated on her serially. The worst case of his cheating was when he was caught in bed with Mary's best friend. The last time he beat her, she was rushed to the hospital, and she was admitted for a week.

She knows the relationship is toxic, but she cannot leave John as she says he is her first love and the only guy that understands her. She told John she was going to quit the relationship if he does not change his attitude towards her and stop his serial cheating. They both opt to see a counselor and John's uncle. After narrating everything to the counselor, he said no relationship is perfect and that Mary should try to be patient with John because he was going to change as he was only exhibiting the traits of a young adult.

Mary was confused after talking with the counselor, but she was more devastated when John's uncle affirmed that any man who sleeps with just one woman isn't strong. He said it can lead to malfunctioning of his hormones if he doesn't taste other ladies out there. He went further to say that abusing Mary is also a sign that John would be able to defend his home well if any issue of security ever happens.

The counselor and John's uncle are examples of flying monkeys.

HOW TO DEAL WITH A FLYING MONKEY

It is terrible how people can be manipulated for several years and abused by the narcissist using the flying monkeys. The following are ways to go out of the domain of the flying monkey and be free.

1. Embrace integrity.

Be committed to the truth every day, so they do not have anything to use against you to blackmail you. Ensure that you are calm always and do not freak out even when there is any disagreement between you and the narcissist, most notably in public places as the narcissist loves to provoke you in the presence of a vast crowd, workplace, or family function when you are with someone who respects you. They will usually try to make you feel like the crazy and challenging person as they will try to use it against you.

2. Opt-out of the relationship.

Ensure there is no more communication between you and the narcissist, block them on every social media channel, on your phone and if they call you, hang up the phone on them and never allow them to say any word to you as they plan to appeal to your emotions and suck supply from you. Also, ensure that you don't communicate with their flying monkeys as the flying monkeys will be used to seduce you back into their fold.

3. Never try to convince them of the truth.

You will never be liberated by believing the narcissist. A naïve victim may try to convince the narcissist to change their attitude because they really do have affection for them and do not want to lose them. The narcissist is never interested in being the right person and does not like the truth, so telling them the truth is a waste of time.

There are times when the flying monkey is a sister, colleague, or roommate, and you can not entirely break off from them. The best method is to avoid sharing relevant information with them as any information shared with them will be shared with the narcissist.

4. And finally, when feasible, go away.

If your next-door neighbor is a flying monkey, and you stay in a small neighborhood, move away from there. For example, if it's in your immediate environment like where you work, you can manage it for some time. You can find out how to create better boundaries, how to put and insist on limits, how to respond instead of reacting, but that's a quick way out. The best option will be to look for a new job, so you don't keep getting drained of energy seeing sycophants every morning who only want the worst to happen to you.'

HOW CAN YOU KNOW IF YOU ARE BEING USED AS A FLYING MONKEY?

1. You become so emotional about the narcissist, even when others says the narcissist did something wrong, you are never patient to hear them and verify if what they said is true or false.

2. You decide to carry the burdens and challenges of the narcissist; you invest your time, money, and resources just for the narcissist to be comfortable and satisfied.

HOW DO YOU AVOID BEING USED AS A FLYING MONKEY?

It's crazy when you discover that a narcissist uses you just to achieve his own personal interest and he has a plan to destroy you someday and abandon you. The narcissist usually takes advantage of people and will never be sorry for their actions. Should you discover that you have been used as a flying monkey and you want to stop being used, you need to consider the following:

1. Never take sides until the truth about any issue has been revealed in any circumstance that involves a narcissist.

2. Critically think about whatever an abuser tells you and never jump to any conclusion. Observe their attitudes and compare them with what they told you.

3. Ask yourself if the story spun by the narcissist about the victim realistic or is the narcissist just trying to paint the victim as terrible and crazy?

4. Be frank in what you do, mind your business, and don't give room for being used as a tool for a narcissist; remember an idle hand is the devil's workshop. A narcissist will always seek an inactive person to use for his next escapade.

Dating
The Narcissist

Chapter 10

Do You Want to Know Why You are Dating a Narcissist?

There exist so many perspectives on why people are so attracted to this kind of person. There are different views from different schools of thoughts that guys who had mommy issues tend to demand a lot of attention from women, and that also applies to ladies who had daddy issues directly or indirectly, knowingly or unknowingly, and we are all looking for some kind of balance in our lives. *What do I mean by this?*

For example, you know someone who is always being abused in a relationship or worse, and you keep advising as a friend that individual to break up the relationship, but they keep refusing. It sometimes isn't really their fault.

There are some psychological issues attached to that act of abuse on the part of the victims. Try to look back into their past, and check the kind of people they have been in a relationship with.

In this chapter, we will aim to understand some of the reasons why we often find ourselves in relationships with egocentric, selfish, and self-loving partners—the narcissist.

Before we get into the real deal, we have to establish some

facts, and you might have come across some of these facts. Sit back and relax!

Let's establish who a narcissist is again

Let's just lay out the facts. A narcissist is someone who has extreme love for himself. He tends to act superior, bossy, successful, and proud.

Narcissists like to be in control of everything around them. They have this idea that the world they live in is imperfect. So they want to make it perfect by bossing everybody around.

They seek power to be in total control, so if they are in some way deprived of that power, they might get aggressive or abusive.

Also, as a narcissist likes to be in control, they never want to be responsible for the outcome. They like people to do what they have in their mind but aren't interested in or are never accountable for the consequences. In simpler words, they are selfish. I am sure you work with one narcissist in your company such that he never agrees with anyone's idea because to him, his opinion is the best. They also tend to have no boundaries at all. They believe that they own everything, and that everything should be done their way.

They get really annoyed or angry anytime someone says no to them. Some people feel they are acting all confident, but that's not it. They will find a means to get that thing they want via cajoling, bargaining, persistence, and demanding to the extent of stealing or taking it by force.

Now that we have successfully established who a narcissist is, we can dive right into the reasons why you are dating a narcissist. However, there are other qualities of a narcissist that might not be mentioned. We would do well to check the internet for more. The main emphasis of this chapter is to lay out the reasons why you are currently in a relationship with a narcissist. There are a lot of explanations for the reasons why you are currently dating someone. It could be because that particular person was always there for you when no one else was. It could be because the person took care of you when you had nothing going. Maybe the person helped you figure life out or helped you with your challenges. There are many other reasons but the reasons why you are currently dating or always dating a narcissist includes the following:

Sexual Attraction

"Not everything that glitters is gold." Sometimes, something terrible for you might just look all good on the outside. When you find yourself intensely sexually attracted to a man or woman, it might take a while before you realize you are with them because of the intense sexual attraction.

That strong sexual attraction for the narcissist has blinded you from seeing the truth.

Seduction

Another thing is that a narcissist is a very skilled type of con-artist. They can manipulate to hook you in. They may be quite a charmer and very seductive.

Some can be great listeners and ethical company that you'd enjoy. They may seduce with their sweet talks, abject attention, and flattery. They are usually self-accomplished, wealthy, powerful, and talented.

All this is enough to impress you and distract you from who they really are.

Familiarity

When a person is abused when very young, in most cases, before they enter the teenage years, there are two ways in which the event affects the individual psychologically.

Either the individual accepts it as something healthy or rejects that action as wrong.

For instance, a young girl who was raped by her uncle when she was just seven years old

She either takes it as a regular thing and starts sleeping with men while growing up or hates men and sees sex as bad generally. This logic also applies here.

Probably you've had a narcissistic parent, and you feel that getting treated that way is a regular thing and there is nothing wrong with it.

This might be a cogent reason why you are in a relationship with a narcissist.

You might have grown to feel that your feelings don't matter, and this makes you really blind when you are poorly treated. Don't blame yourself for that.

Vulnerability

The last and most important reason is vulnerability.

There is an example of a little girl who was always bullied when she was in high school.

Even though she was very bright, she wasn't critical to people, both her teachers and peers. She felt tossed around and eventually after trying to stand up for her self one day she got so severely beaten that she almost ended up losing her legs.

So she made a promise to herself that she would excel at her studies, and one day become a boss. She ended up becoming a jerk of a boss.

This is kind of like what we're talking about here.

What was your childhood like? How horrible was it?

A relationship with a narcissist always follows three stages: **Idealization, Devaluation, and The Discard Stage.**

IDEALIZATION STAGE

A narcissist firstly searches for the target and makes them feel so important. The victims are usually beautiful, intelligent, maybe luxurious or classy. They typically have something great as a means to boost the narcissist's ego and status. They give all the attention they seek, such that the victim has the idea of them as perfect. The victim starts to feel like they are soulmates. I call this stage the fake stage. It usually takes a couple of months. Long enough to get the victim hooked on love and affection. Little do they know what is coming next.

DEVALUATION STAGE

In this stage, the narcissist just switches. They withdraw all the attention they have been giving you and become really silent. No calls or texts for weeks. They only gradually disappear and act all busy. They tend to be aggressive when you question their behavior. They could even blame you for it. They started becoming annoyed with you. You begin to wonder what you did. What happened was that he doesn't need you again.

DISCARD STAGE

Most narcissistic individuals end up leaving their partners wondering what they did wrong. They just hop up and leave their partner in an emotional mess. The victims begin to ask themselves several questions like: What did I do wrong? Was I the cause of the breakup?

Chapter 11

An Important Question - Am I Dating a Narcissist?

This is one of the most critical questions in a relationship. Along with questions like, *"Am I dating the right person?"* and *"Am I comfortable in my relationship?"* and many other issues.

It is imperative to stay happy and healthy, both physically and emotionally, in any relationship. There are stories of different people coming from a bad relationship with psychological breakdown. Yes, it is true. This is why the question *"Am I dating a Narcissist?"* is essential and paramount because being in a relationship with a narcissist is a terrible choice.

It might be your worst choice in life. This is another scenario for you. You know when someone is appropriately dressed, walking tall on the street and happy with himself. People keep staring at him, and he thinks they probably think of him as handsome. Suddenly, a beautiful young lady walks up to him and tells him he has dog poop on the back of his shirt. Suddenly, his countenance will change, realizing why those people had been staring at him like that. This is like what this chapter is going to do.

It is going to enlighten you, shedding more light on who you are dating. Sometimes, you might not see something until it's too late. The association is one of the most delicate topics, and it'd be unfortunate to joke about it because it could affect all other aspects of your life.

Here, we are going to list out the common signs on how to identify a narcissist. It is high time, and we avoided those who're out to disrupt our peace. After several years of reading and studying several psychology materials on personality disorder, psychologists have gained a lot of insight into who a narcissistic individual is and how to identify them. There are some aspects of their behavior that is complicated and hard to understand.

In a lazy man's tone, it is just weird. Do you want to know a little definition for narcissists? They are **silent killers** or **slow poison**. They gradually kill you little by little without you realizing the damage they've done to you.

Some people might be thinking a narcissistic individual is psychologically disturbed. No, not really! You won't see them on the streets, homeless, in rags, or begging. They are always well-to-do and self-accomplished. It's hard to tell if they are a narcissist or not. These few commons signs would help you know if you are currently in a relationship with a narcissist or not. If after reading through this chapter you notice you are in a relationship with one, please pack your bags and run for your life. Don't try to change them because it may be complicated. Note that some individuals may have one of these signs listed below, but it doesn't mean they are narcissists. Please read carefully and digest properly.

ELEVEN SIGNS YOU ARE IN A RELATIONSHIP WITH A NARCISSIST

In chapter one, we talked a little about the common signs to look out for in your partner. Here we are going to be shedding more light on that aspect. It is left for you to make the decision and take the necessary steps if you are a victim. If you are not, try as much as possible to avoid them. Run, if possible.

1. VERY CHARMING AND PERSUASIVE AT

FIRST

You meet this very handsome and rich guy. He treats you very specially, says very loving things to you and makes you feel good about yourself. That's how a narcissist gets their prey. He's quite the catch in the beginning. You almost could say in the first two to three months that he's your soulmate or heaven-sent angel. Suddenly all that stops, and you feel distant and unloved. According to great psychologists, narcissists are very skilled in love bombing their victims for some time. They are what we call, "too good to be true" kind of people. They seem like better lovers than those who actually love you when it comes to gifting, calling, texting, infatuations, and sweet-talking. In my two-years relationship with a narcissist, at first, he was so charming and sweet. My parents knew him quite well to the extent my dad took him as his son. They go out on weekends at times to fish. All this happened only at the beginning of the relationship.

2. SELF-CENTEREDNESS

After the first lovey-dovey stage they feel you are hooked on love. They start to showcase their true self. This is one of the primary attributes, and you then you see self-centeredness. They act selfish. They think of only themselves. They don't say, "oh! I went by the grocery store, and I got you this or that." No, they only care about themselves and not you. On the outside, while anyone that matter is watching, they are very attentive and supportive, but when it is just you, they switch. So when you complain to your friends, they'll think you're crazy to the extent that you think you're insane too.

3. PERFECTIONIST

A narcissist never goes for people who are not accomplished in one way. They don't choose mediocrely; they actually study their victims before going after them. You've to be something before they can approach you: beautiful, a sport or music star, a successful businesswoman, and the list continues. It is always something that would boost their ego or social status. So, while in a relationship with a narcissist, the focus is not on the growth of the relationship. The focus of a narcissist is on their outward image. What people think of them as a power/perfect couple. This is because they like to protect their public image.

4. BOSSY

When you first started dating, they loved every damn thing about you. Your love for rap music, funny reality TV shows, country music, partying, and other things. I mean everything. It seemed like he was the perfect guy for you. Suddenly, they begin to boss you around. They suddenly want you to start living the way they want. They believe if you are not doing things the way they want, you're wrong. You begin to wonder whether you were the one who caused their change or if they have some other lady on the side.

5. THE NEVER-WRONG ATTITUDE

It is somewhat impossible to argue with a narcissist. After a while of arguing, you may get confused. This is because they are under the impression that they are never wrong. They are always right. That opinion of theirs is the best and only option for you. So arguing with them on a matter is impossible.

6. LACK OF EMPATHY

Now, this part is the saddest. It is quite different from when you see a sad movie, and you don't cry. It is way different from that. A narcissist isn't capable of empathizing with others or you as his partner. He simply doesn't care. All the cares they showered on you at the beginning of the relationship were fake and timely. Don't try to change them because they cannot change. Just opt out!

7. LASHING OUT

When they notice you might leave them, they begin to become sweet again. Of course, they don't want you to leave them. When they get the feeling that you are beginning to do without them, they may get angry and lash out at you. They start to blame you for pulling away from them emotionally, bringing on one excuse or the other. They may lie if necessary.

8. THEY MAKE YOU FEEL BAD ABOUT YOURSELF

After the first stage of love bombing their partner, a narcissist switches their behavior and starts to make you feel like a wrong person. All the things he was okay with before, he suddenly hates, and now, you are the bad person.

Maybe he used to be cool with you buying Chinese when you are too tired to cook. Suddenly, he hates fast food and accuses you of starving him always.

9. COMPLIMENTS

They love compliments from others. It feeds their ego. When you continuously compliment them as a sweet partner, they love it.

10. NO TRUE FRIENDS

Narcissists never have real friends. They have colleagues all around, business partners and acquaintances. They actually choose their cliques based on their needs. They don't actually keep real friends. So, when you go out with your friends, they tend to get angry and feel left out. They start to criticize you for the kinds of friends you're hanging out with.

11. YOU FEEL LIKE A THING

At a point in the relationship with a narcissist, you suddenly get a feeling you are being used. He just gets what he wants: sex, food, and so on. You are neglecting your own needs. He doesn't even compliment you again, like how beautiful you're, how successful you are becoming, and so on.

I sincerely hope you are not dating a narcissist because it's a toxic relationship. With all these signs written above, you can see that dating a narcissist is not a good thing in any way. They don't actually think they are doing anything wrong so it may be impossible to save them. It's best to look out for yourself and find a way out. Well, stay sharp and follow this section of the book carefully as I would also be providing you insights on how you can do that.

Chapter 12

The Signs that You are Dating a Narcissist

Since the beginning of this part of the book, how to recognize a narcissist has been emphasized, so that with all this information, you can avoid falling victim. Another reason is to help you realize if you are already caught up in their nest. In shorter words, a victim.

In the previous chapters, we talked about who a narcissist is. From there, you caught a glimpse of or had an idea of who they are. We then went ahead to elaborate a little on the few common signs that will help you recognize a narcissist.

In this chapter, we want to talk exclusively on the symptoms you see when or if you are in a relationship with a narcissist.

Firstly, a narcissist undoubtedly needs you to supply their needs. They don't want to love you for who you are. They only wish to use you for their selfish reasons.

They need you to do some things for them. The funniest thing is that you can never understand this unless you are an expert on dealing with a narcissist or have knowledge of their existence.

If you are ignorant about them, you'll keep blaming yourself for what isn't your fault. Throughout the time of dating a narcissist, you will have no idea what they are doing to you.

You might have a good job and be independent until the narcissist comes along. At first, you might perceive them as ambitious, caring, charming, always there for you at the right time and attractive, to say the least. You'd never know that you are falling into a bottomless hole.

As the days roll by, your love for them will only grow stronger, and for the first few weeks, you would feel great until "the war" begins.

This chapter's primary emphasis is on two things. The first thing is to help those who have no experience dating and are about to enter a relationship to recognize that some relationships are bad for them.

You need to look at these signs and check the person you want to date. This will save you a lot of stress, both physically and emotionally.

The second thing is to help people who are currently in a relationship to recognize whether their partner is a narcissist or not.

Take a look at another scenario, a little girl, let's say six-years-old, always receives letters from her dad every year on her birthday.

Anytime she asks of her dad from her mom, her mom would tell her, he was working in another state and that he was swamped. She actually believed what her mom said. She didn't know her mom didn't know her dad. She was just trying to protect her from the truth. When she got to see this, she didn't fall for that lie again. That's what ignorance does to you: it keeps you locked up in a cage, but when you know the truth, you are free.

Before the signs are explained, you must be clear of the fact that a narcissist has no idea they are doing anything. They feel just okay, like how you think about yourself.

So, they don't think anything is wrong with them, and they certainly won't consider seeing a psychiatrist.

Let's dive in!

A narcissist thinks the world revolves around them. It is all about what they want, or need, not a collective want or need.

For example, a narcissistic man may wish his partner to stay at home as his housewife, even though he knows she is a successful businesswoman. He just wants to have his way, also though it may be irrational at times.

The woman may try to please him by staying at home and forsaking her years of labor and hard work, not knowing that he was acting based on his selfish reasons. He thinks his opinions should be the only option in the relationship. He may tell the woman she should not associate with friends of hers again, even childhood friends.

When the woman refuses, he may pull some stunts to the extent of asking her to choose between him and her friends and ignorantly, the woman might dismiss her friends.

The most dangerous thing about a narcissistic man is that they are what ladies are dying to get. They are charismatic, fun to be around, rich, handsome, naturally fit, maybe famous and so on.

They are better than those who genuinely love you and want you for good. This is the worst! They are even better at wooing because they have better resources than the other guy who genuinely loves you.

The essence of what's here is that if you were to choose between a narcissist and a guy who truly loves you, you'd select the narcissist. They are the "too-good-to-be-true" kind of boyfriends.

You know when you are about to kill a chicken, you feed it well with good food and water. This is kind of like how a narcissistic relationship looks.

Note that all these kind gestures and over-loving behaviors are to deceive you. That's not really who they are. At first, they want the things you want out of life; you seem to have the same likes and beliefs. You are delighted that finally, you found your perfect match. After a few months or a year into the relationship, they switch into a total jerk such that you begin to wonder. They turn into an absolute monster. They start to treat you like trash, disrespect you, embarrass you, be mean to you and are also very harsh. It's not your fault, it's just their nature.

A narcissist isn't accountable for anything. They are cunning and manipulative. For instance, maybe you brought something to their attention. They disprove that idea outright and tell you what to do until you agree with them, and when the negative consequences of their opinions show up, they deny it and find a way to blame you for it.

That's just crazy, right? How could this be possible? But it's genuine. If you can relate to what has been said so far, say enough is enough. You need to be free of this emotional disturbance you call a relationship.

When you are in a relationship with a narcissist, you always feel like you need to check your behavior every blessed day. They find a way to reduce your self-esteem such that you depend on them for anything. Remember, you no longer hang out with your best friends. They did that! They turned your back to them. So, you have no one to turn to for advice. You only have the narcissist.

That's who a narcissist is. They isolate you from anybody who can influence you positively. They make you feel dependent in a way that you think you are lucky to have them in your life.

Another example for the women: maybe you tell him that you don't appreciate the way he flirts with other women. He would say to you that you are the reason why he does that. That you never have time for him, as you are always hanging out with your work colleagues. He could also tell you that you are never satisfied with anything he does. That you are the reason why your previous relationships ended up in a mess.

You tend to destroy everything with your silly emotions. In

one way, he reduces your esteem; he makes you feel guilty. I don't think any woman deserves to go through all this at all. Another way you know a narcissist is that they treat you like they detest you, but at the same time they treat you like they need you a lot. Funny, right?

They disrespect you, embarrasses you, treat you harshly, but at the same time, they don't want you to leave. That's a narcissist! It is not because they love you.

They don't love you or want to treat you right, but they don't want any other person to treat you right either.

You might even plead for them to change, as you cry or feel sad, you are continually feeding their narcissistic supply, so they wouldn't want you to leave.

As soon as you decide to leave them, they can do anything to get you back.

They may use guilt, fear, your parents, they may buy you beautiful things or show glitches of what it was initially at the beginning of the relationship.

They'll try their very best to be persuasive just to get you back.

The only way they will leave you is when they find another person just like you that can replace you. When they find someone else to replace you, they discard you.

Every man and woman needs to know these signs we have been talking about. When they see, they start to see things differently. They know what to avoid and what to take in.

If you are already a victim, don't panic, this book is adequately packaged for you. Stay calm as we carefully walk you down a path to healing from a narcissist.

Chapter 13
Narcissistic Date Vs. Healthy Date

We all know how dating goes. Two people meet somehow, it could be on social media, at a bar or on a dating site. They go on several dates, have fun, have sex or not, and eventually, some chose to commit to serious relationships while others just go their separate ways. Dating is not really a biggie. What's dangerous about dating is that most times, you meet a complete stranger who you don't know the background of and start to fall in love. As scary as that may sound, on a brighter side, a lot of people have met their soulmates via the same process. That kind of puts our minds at rest.

We've been talking a lot about narcissists since the beginning of this book, and in this chapter, we are going to differentiate between a regular healthy date and a narcissistic date. Trust me, there is always a difference. If you aren't familiar with narcissists, you may not be able to spot the differences. With this chapter, you will be able to know the difference between them.

A date is meant for two people to get to know each other accurately. It either ends well or not. There is always a conversation between the two parties where they get to talk about several issues.

You will probably never have been on any date where there

was no conversation. That's probably weird. If you ever go on a date with someone that doesn't want to talk at all, you should run. Maybe they are a serial killer or something! On a more serious note, there is always a conversation where you get to decide whether he's charming or she's sweet or something terrible.

During a date with a narcissist, you'll notice that all attention is focused on him/her. Instead of a conversation, you have a monologue in which only one person talks. Dates can be terrible at times, but this is the worst kind.

A healthy date will involve a lovely conversation between the two parties. The funny thing about this is that most people will fall for a narcissist because of the beautiful things they say about themselves. They might start by talking about their previous relationships, how crazy they were, then to how successful they are presently, and so on.

During a date with a narcissist, whenever you raise any topic, they will find a way to make the topic about themselves. They are always on about themselves without having any regard for the other person. Most people will overlook this because the narcissist seems funny and charismatic.

A reasonable healthy date involves both parties talking about their past. It may be weird, sad, or funny, which makes it interesting. There is some kind of sharing in a healthy date.

However, a narcissistic date involves the narcissist, instead of sharing, lectures the other party about their own life alone, totally neglecting the other person. At the end of every date, no matter how charming a person might seem, try as much as possible to think over the date.

On a regular date, the two parties try to impress each other. They try to be on their best behavior just to make sure everything was perfect

Narcissists are egocentric individuals. They may complain about the waiter not carrying out their job adequately, give them a reduced tip, or try to make a scene, drawing all the attention to themselves. They never seem to agree with anyone, and they believe that they should be the only option. Some ladies may find this sexy; that's why they fall victim to narcissists.

This may not be the best way to differentiate a narcissistic date from a healthy date. Some men may act like this, but they may not be narcissists. They are just impatient individuals who have no time for nonsense.

A healthy date might entail one or other person making a reservation for two at a good restaurant where they sit and enjoy themselves. On the other hand, there is a narcissistic date. The date may start with the narcissist quarreling with the manager of the restaurant on their seating arrangement.

Don't forget that narcissists are usually self-accomplished and successful individuals. So money may not be their problem. They may demand you sit in another location because they don't like where they are seated.

During a date with a narcissistic individual, they might start to complain a lot about their present condition, career and job, and life in general.

You know when on a date, you might get a call or need to reply to a message from a colleague or someone important to you. If you are on a healthy date, a partner may not mind as long as you give an excuse.

A narcissist won't allow that one because they want all the attention to be focused on them. They are probably talking about themselves, and don't want your attention to be distracted. So any slight distraction may get them annoyed.

Let's just assume that the dates we've been talking about went beyond only mere dates and led to something serious like a relationship.

Dating a narcissist can be really demanding. In a good and healthy relationship, both parties have their roles to play. It is more or less like a joint agreement between two people. They both have a say in the relationship. They do things together, go on outings together, do romantic stuff and all other sorts of things.

A narcissistic relationship, on the other hand, is quite different from that. In a narcissistic relationship, only one person's opinion matters. A narcissist is usually very manipulative, so it is almost impossible to win an argument with them. They bend your decision to what they want.

Maybe you are thinking of buying new clothing material for a program, for example. Let's say the color of the material is red. They can tell you to buy blue because blue goes with the car they are taking to the occasion.

In such a scenario, they actually know that red is one of your favorite colors, but they will find a way to manipulate you into choosing blue.

A normal healthy relationship usually entails the two lovers always expressing their emotions through calls, texts, romantic getaways, and several outings with friends. A narcissistic relationship is entirely different from that.

It starts with a powerful connection between the so-called lovers, and suddenly, there is a withdrawal by the narcissist.

They no longer call or text. They act like they were swamped at work; that's why they didn't call or text you. After a while, you begin to feel alone most of the time such that you will be the one calling and texting them. At this point, you feel very dependent on them.

When you finally gather the courage to talk to them about what you noticed, they blame you for it, and you begin to feel sad and ask for their forgiveness.

You see how difficult it is for someone to date a narcissist. You end up being messed up emotionally. They don't want to know your friends talk less about going out with them. However, you must know their colleagues at work or whoever they hang with.

Before dating anyone make sure you double-check all these things we've been talking about. It is paramount to be able to spot a toxic relationship before it even starts. That's one of the reasons why this book exists: to make sure people don't suffer from these narcissistic individuals again.

Note that healthy relationships are built on trust and equal respect for one another, not the other way round. In a healthy relationship, there are times where you show empathy as a sign of love. There are times where you make compromises and so on. A narcissistic relationship is void of all these. It's mainly about one person, the narcissist. Everyone deserves to be respected.

If you ever find yourself in any relationship where you don't feel comfortable it is advisable to exit ASAP. This brings us to our next chapter, where we will discuss the things a narcissist will say to get you back when you eventually decide to leave them.

I hope you are learning.

Chapter 14

Six Sneaky Things Narcissists Do to Get You Back

We have learned a lot about how to recognize a narcissist; the signs you will notice while on a date with a narcissist; how they will first make you feel good in the first few months and then start to maltreat you afterwards.

We have also learned that narcissists are con artists and are fraudulent in behavior. What do I mean by this? What I mean is that they act like a person they are not at the beginning of the relationship and switch up at some point in the relationship.

In this chapter, we are going to learn something different. Many people have been in relationships with a narcissist without an idea that they are actually being abused.

Like it was stated earlier, that narcissists are like con artists, they are cunning and very persuasive when they need something.

No matter how the victims try to leave the relationship, they always find ways to suck them back. A narcissist will mistreat you, neglect you and do all sorts of horrible things, but the moment you decide to leave they suddenly become remorseful and apologetic.

This is one of the most dangerous parts of a narcissistic relationship. You may think they have repented and will change for the better, but they will not.

Learning to recognize them is not enough to avoid them. You have to know their tricks as well. When you are familiar with all the methods of a con artist, he can no longer blackmail you with anything.

After a series of bad treatment and abuse in a narcissistic relationship, the victim decides to leave. This is when the narcissists will start to behave well and sweet again. Don't fall for it! It is just a scheme to make you stay in the relationship. It is called *"hoovering"* like the vacuum cleaner.

They are not trying to get you back into the relationship because they want to treat you right. They are only doing that because he wants to keep treating you like trash.

It is a method narcissists use to keep their victims from leaving them. It is just like when someone is deep into a cult, and they are unable to leave.

So let's quickly dive into the seven sneaky things a narcissist will probably do or say to keep you locked up in their cage.

   1. *Counseling*

The first most common excuse they use is counseling. As we all know that advice is well-known for solving relationship problems.

Every person now has a counselor who they talk to every now and then when they encounter problems.

Try talking to someone about your relationship issue; the first thing they would advise you to do is to go for counseling with your partner. They might probably refer you to a counselor who has helped them at some point or another.

When a narcissist sees that you are about to leave, they may come and say, *"Hey babe, I thought a lot about what you said last night. I am willing to change for good because I love you and I want this to work. I've decided to go to counseling."*

When the victim hears this statement, they become happy.

2. Cheating

Whenever you catch a narcissist cheating on you, they will try to find a way to keep you by accepting their fault and ridiculing themselves.

They may say, *"Baby, I am a fool for cheating on you."*

They may later bring up some cock and bull story that will win your heart back.

They may say something like, *"I met him/her when we weren't together, and now they don't want to leave me alone."*

They will say just about anything to make sure they get you back. Don't fall for this! Although it's tough to leave when you're in love with a narcissist, unfortunately.

3. Friends

When they have tried every possible thing to get you back, they may try to be friends with you.

"Since you don't want to accept me back, can we be friends?"

They don't want to treat you right. At the same time, they don't want anybody to make you happy either.

Narcissists generally and gradually suck the life out of you. If you have been in a relationship with a narcissist, and they are trying to get you back with this line avoid it and move on! You don't need them. What is crazy about narcissists is that they are capable of hiding their real personality for a reasonably long time. Spotting them quickly may be very hard.

So after a while of being your friend, they become charming and sweet again to the extent that they buy you gifts and try to seduce you all over again.

They are good actors; they can fake their emotions anytime any day, just to deceive you.

4. "The Only One"

In most cases, women fall victims of this trick. When you eventually pack your bags to leave his house, that's when he pulls out this trick.

Narcissists can lie with a straight face and no facial expression. Remember, narcissistic individuals are not capable of showing empathy or love. They only love themselves.

They only show compassion sometimes at the beginning of the relationship and when you try to leave.

After a narcissist sees that you are in love, he starts to abuse you in all kinds of ways.

He neglects your emotions, disrespects you, embarrasses you, and ignores your opinion on anything. But when you decide to leave, they can say stuff like, *"you know you are the only one for me."*

5. *"I'll Make it up to you."*

You have tried everything to make the relationship work, but they kept abusing your rights in the relationship, and now you are really upset.

You eventually decide to break up with them, and that's when you hear something like,

"Hey Babe, you know I love you, I promise to make it up to you."

You must be wondering how this kind of words can keep the victim in the relationship.

People are generally empathetic, loving, and adorable beings. Once they're in love with someone, it is not easy for them to give up on them. As long as the abusers are persuasive and apologetic, they will accept you back.

A narcissist is highly skilled when it comes to this, just to deceive the victim.

6. *"Something Touched Me"*

That moment the victim is trying to leave the narcissist, they suddenly repent and starts to apologize and say things like,

"I think I had an encounter. Something touched me, and I realize all I have been to you..."

As a result of the love they have, the victim will forgive them not knowing what is coming next.

What the narcissist is trying to do is play on the victim's emotions and deceive them with apologies.

Deep down, the narcissist doesn't care about you.

Never think that crying or making sad faces will make a narcissist change. They are just out to hurt vulnerable people who will fall under their spell.

Now that you have learned about the six common sneaky tricks a narcissist can use to get you back you can now easily catch them anytime there's need. There is more to come.

Chapter 15

LIES

*W*henever Nicole thinks back to her childhood days, she smiles. It wasn't easy to grow up the way she did. Her family wasn't close. No family dinner or outings, just a bunch of people trying to live each day, one at a time.

She had to go to school at the tail end of the hood. No one influenced her because she was pretty much on her own during elementary school. She only had her bicycle and arithmetic to think of.

High school, of course, entails a lot of peer pressure. She couldn't fit into any clique, not the cool kids, not the dancers, not the sports team or the cheerleaders. She was just weird.

Unlike every other teenager, lying wasn't her thing. She didn't have reason to lie. She didn't have to rest for going to a party because she was never invited to one, or maybe to dances or movies because no one asked her out.

When she finds out someone had lied to her, she felt hurt, betrayed, and deceived, and may not be able to trust the person again.

Is lying a good or bad thing?

Well, what about the old tale about a young man?

There is a famous tale of a young man who once ran into the village and shouted that a lion was coming and that everybody should run.

The villagers, on hearing this awful message, left their houses and started to run into the bush only to discover it was a prank or a lie per se.

On another day, that young man came again with the same story about the lion. Unfortunately, this time, it was true. They didn't believe him, so the lion came and destroyed the village leaving a lot of people dead.

But that is enough of stories. They were just to lay out some facts.

It is no longer a new thing to state that narcissists are skilled liars and with their other awful characteristics or qualities, they play their common sneaky tricks to get you back when you decide to leave and lots more.

Narcissists are sneaky bastards with a confident look. So lying is part of their lives.

They lie for so many reasons; at the same time, they can rest for no reason. Since they intend to hurt you, lying is not a problem for them. If you are in a relationship with a narcissist, you may never know if they were lying or not. You believe them because you love them.

Sometimes, a narcissist may tell you that they are lying, to see you get hurt or cry, and they blame you for it. They are not good people in any way. They want to prey on your weakness and vulnerability. I've said it and will always say, narcissists don't deserve any love from you.

However, deep down beyond all the confidence, fame, and egocentrism, they are low-esteemed individuals. All that outward impression is just a cover-up, but you would never know because they are highly skilled manipulators.

Narcissists lie for a lot of reasons. They lie to keep victims hooked in the relationship.

We've seen some of their lies in our previous chapter. They can lie just to deceive you from seeing what's going on and many other reasons like that. Although, some may say, men lie and generally cheat whenever they are in a relationship. Does that mean all men are narcissists? No!

Absolutely not. Firstly, not all men lie or cheat on their spouses or girlfriends.

That's a wrong mentality to carry about. The same way there are faithful women out there, there are also faithful men as well. You probably just fall for the lying and cheating men because you don't know the game.

For instance, some ladies have a soft spot for hot guys with the muscles, abs, and all. They don't really pay attention to other important details one should know. So they fall victim quickly.

WHY DO NARCISSISTS LIE?

Narcissists lie for a lot of reasons. They lie to get you emotionally attached to them.

You know when you started dating, they were sweet, charming, loving, and romantic. They send your favorite flower to your office every morning.

They appreciated you so much by telling you good things about yourself. Sorry to tell you that, those were all lies.

They were just buttering you up with a sweet flavor that will later melt really badly.

They lie to get some kind of emotional feedback from you. Either to get you to trust them, make you feel dependent on them, or to make you feel sad and frustrated. Nothing good comes out of it. They also lie to ensure they are still in control of your life. Narcissists live in a different world of their own.

They don't believe in the saying that goes like, **"together we can build"** or **"united we stand."** They always want to stand on their own.

Sometimes, they lie to get the upper hand just as a means of gaining control. At the beginning of this book, we said narcissists are never accountable for anything. When it comes to claiming responsibility for anything, they avoid it. Narcissists, after a long time of lying, develop such a lying habit that they can't do without it. They become so good at it such that it is almost impossible to detect. As said earlier, they are manipulators. They try to manipulate every situation in their favor.

Lying is one of the ways they use to ensure that. Sometimes, it's all a game to them. They want to see how you will react. They like to see how it will all play out when they fabricate a story. Trust me; when they lie, they have the resources to back up that lie. They have everything all planned out just to manipulate you. The most painful thing in all this is that many victims are too blind to see this in them. That's why they fall victim.

COMMON LIES THEY TELL

1. She/he seduced me

When you catch a narcissist cheating, they never admit their faults. Instead, they blame whoever they were cheating with.

"She seduced me,"

"He made me do it."

"How do you expect me to react when I was seduced?"

"It wasn't my fault."

They never like to be responsible for anything whatsoever.

2. Do you believe in love at first sight?

This lie is pervasive when they just started dating you.

They come at you with lines like this to lure you into a toxic relationship with zero benefits. They don't mean any of that.

Another line could be, **"we have so much in common."**

3. I can never lie to you

When they utter this statement, it means everything they said earlier is a total lie from the bottom of hell. In fact, they just deceived you blatantly.

4. I'm just checking on you

They say this very often to keep you in check to ensure they are still in control of the relationship. They are just checking in to see if you actually miss them or want them. They love that attention.

5. *I hate cheating*

When any man or woman says these three words in a relationship, start to suspect something.

Well, if you trust your man or woman, you have no problem.

Narcissists are far different from ordinary people. They will cheat on you and expect you not to cheat too. This is so hurtful. They are out there getting the grove from different people, they deprive you of that affection and make sure you don't do what they are doing.

6. *I'm now a changed man*

When you suddenly decide to leave him, they come up with statements like this. It's a lie. He's not changed at all. He just doesn't want you to leave him.

He can also utter statements like, *"I hate myself for what I did."*

Being involved in a relationship with a narcissistic individual is a crazy ride that can land you in a series of therapy sessions. The only way to solve this is opting out. They don't deserve your compromise, love, or your affection.

They just meddle with it and spit it in your face. Regardless of what they do to keep you hooked, **IT'S NOT LOVE!**.

It is merely an everyday supply of vitality that you provide for them whether you need it or not.

Chapter 16

Dating Tips

In a new relationship, it is possible for your partner to show some signs of narcissism but not to the extreme. When the flags are becoming very strong, that is when there is a problem. However, we must understand that some people display signs of narcissism who are happily married today. So, it's not entirely a bad idea to date someone who shows little signs of narcissism.

Most especially when you both are so deep into the relationship, there are certain tricks we can use to deal with them, but only if the connection is not toxic or abusive.

If the relationship is toxic and abusive, then the only solution is to save yourself.

We've been talking about how to recognize narcissists, the signs and symptoms they showcase from the beginning right to the point when they start showing their true identity.

Presently, how to recognize a narcissistic relationship is understood correctly.

If you can't recall correctly, you can refer back to the previous chapters. One thing we left out is that some people might not like to leave their partners even if they show some signs that point towards the fact that they might be narcissists.

This is very understandable! This is not because they don't like themselves, but because of something more profound.

In this chapter, we are going to be discussing some dating or relationship tips. Before we dive into the dating tips, I would like to discuss the concept of ***"healthy narcissism."***

Healthy narcissists are also full of self-love, but they are not emotionally detached like unhealthy narcissists. They have that egocentric behavior, but they do not totally cut themselves off emotionally from their spouse or partner.

This is to say, although they have their selfish desire, you are still relevant to them. Let us see the common differences between healthy narcissism and unhealthy narcissism briefly.

HEALTHY NARCISSISM VS UNHEALTHY NARCISSISM

Healthy narcissists are full of self-confidence in a rational sense. They do not go beyond the average level of self-esteem. Let us see an excellent example in the corporate scene, in a company's board meeting where all the board members gather to make some decisions on some projects.

The company's director needs to appoint someone who would head the projects. The healthy narcissist can get up and talk for himself, saying, *'I believe I can head this project with all confidence.'* An unhealthy narcissist, on the other hand, may get up saying, *'I think we can all agree that I'm the best man to head this project.'*

Can you spot the difference between these two individuals? The first individual has an egocentric attitude to a rational point while the other individual believes he's the only one in the company qualified to head the project. This implies he does not care about the other candidates qualified for that position. He portrays an unrealistic and irrational sense of superiority.

Healthy narcissists love power. They enjoy being in charge or control of something. The other thing they love is likeability and they will do all they can to pursue that power. They can do unsavoury things to be in control: lie, manipulate, and so on.

But healthy narcissists also show genuine concern for other people.

Therefore, if you are in a relationship with one, you are safe.

They never devalue other people or exploit their vulnerability.

Unhealthy narcissists only show concern when they are trying to lure you into a relationship with them.

They do not really care about anything except themselves. When they see you are sincerely in love, they turn into complete jerks. They disrespect you and exploit your vulnerability without any remorse.

When you know a healthy narcissist, that is who they are. They do not change behavior or attitude, unlike unhealthy narcissists.

Unhealthy narcissists constantly change when they get bored. They do not have any particular pattern of living their lives. One minute they are acting all sweet and charming, while at another time they act as if they hate you.

Now that we know that there are healthy narcissists and unhealthy narcissists, we can easily differentiate between them.

RELATIONSHIP TIPS WHENEVER YOU FIND YOURSELF IN A NARCISSISTIC RELATIONSHIP

The first thing to do when you feel you are in this condition is to look back on how you got into the relationship.

Then, you can judge yourself on whether the relationship has damaged your life or not. Maybe you were a successful person before you got into a relationship with them, but now you are some kind of lowly person who depends on them.

You need to get out now!

After doing this and you feel the relationship is not salvageable, here are a few pieces of relationship advice that can help you manage.

Narcissistic Supply

There is something called *'narcissistic supply'*, which narcissists have.

Narcissistic supply has been mentioned earlier on.

Narcissists regularly feed on compliments and praise of others.

If you are the kind of partner who regularly feeds their egocentric attitude, then you need to reduce it to a healthy level. It is more like giving a kid a lot of chocolate. As you consistently give it to them, their thirst for that thing will increase. You can also liken it to drug addiction. Yeah! That is a great example. Retract your steps a little and stop contributing to his narcissism. Look for a way to change that attitude of praising them for whatever they do.

High Level of Denial

Most narcissists are always in denial about their attitude. They are never accountable for any of their actions. They do not believe that whatever they did is their fault. They always blame others for their wrongdoings.

Don't be too emotional or get hurt, that's their nature, and they will not realize what they are doing until you point it out to them. Whenever you notice this act, bring it to their attention. Note that they will definitely not agree with you on anything. Therefore, you have to find a means to change that attitude.

Emotional Check

Put your emotions in check and avoid pouring it out on them. That is precisely what they want, so they can reduce your esteem and devalue you.

Be calm with them whenever you want to point their

attention to something they did to hurt you. For instance, maybe they are always spending too much time away and less time with you. Know how to tell them without giving them room to devalue you.

Seek Professional Help

This should have been the first tip because it is essential.

A professional and experienced therapist will give you ideas on how to handle his behavior better. The same way therapists solve marital problems in healthy relationships, he/she can check out your condition and give you certain tricks.

You will agree with me that some individuals, although not all narcissists, are out to hurt people. So examine them thoroughly and check for their willingness to change.

Chapter 17
Healing After Dating a Narcissist

The stages a relationship with a narcissist goes through have been discussed in the first part of this book. The narcissist identifies their victim and goes after them. They then try to sugarcoat the relationship with great charm and a sweet attitude for the first few months or weeks of the relationship.

After they have discovered that you are so in love with them, their behavior starts to change gradually. All the things you liked together suddenly become disliked by them. They start acting like a complete jerk, drawing away from you emotionally. Then you begin to feel sad and frustrated, and that makes their behavior even crazier such that they disrespect and devalue your image.

After this stage, we have the "***discarding stage***" where the narcissist leaves you for no reason. Then you begin to wonder what went wrong.

Maybe you were even trying to fix what you thought was the problem, or you think you are the problem. Well, congratulations to you! You just survived a toxic relationship, and what's next after the survival of such an unhealthy relationship is healing.

We can liken this type of situation to soldiers who went to

fight in a war.

They face a lot, and most of them usually suffer from Post-Traumatic Stress Disorder (PTSD).

You actually went to battle in your relationship with a narcissist. Most times, when people come out of a narcissistic relationship, they are always so hurt and broken to the extent of vowing never to love again.

Firstly, tell yourself that it wasn't your fault in any way.

Refrain from blaming yourself.

After you have done that correctly, we can move on to the five steps that can help in healing after dating a narcissist.

This narcissistic relationship could go on for years. No matter the number of years, once the narcissist gets bored, they will just leave without saying goodbye. So mean, right?

The five core steps to healing after abuse are:

Support Groups

After coming out of this crazy toxic relationship, you shouldn't stay alone.

You are prone to depression, anxiety, and PTSD at this point as you might find yourself crying and thinking whatever happened was all your fault.

You need to stay around people who will support you during this period.

You can find a support group nearby that you will attend every week. Don't forget you are not the only one that has passed through traumatic experiences.

Getting together with a group of people with similar cases will help you heal better.

Two heads are better than one. And a burden shared is a burden reduced.

In support groups, you can share your problems with different people with similar traumatic experiences such as rape victims, orphans, alcoholics, drug addicts, and so on. Apart from finding a support group, you can also visit a therapist, life coach, or counselor.

You need a therapist with experience handling similar cases to yours. This is very paramount because if the therapist has never dealt with a victim of a narcissistic relationship, he may cause more harm than good. To be on the safe side, get a therapist that has the necessary experience and expertise to guide you through this healing period.

Self Love

Self-love has been known to help victims of different kinds of abuse recover and rediscover their best selves.

Involve yourself in several activities that will help you move on.

Take yourself out, eat healthily, have fun with your friends, indulge yourself with anything good for your mind, body, and spirit.

Involve yourself in sporting activities like lawn tennis, squash, or bicycling.

Some other people may recommend yoga sessions or relaxation centers such as the spa, and so on.

You can also get books like this that will help speed up the healing process. Another thing is to get yourself busy with something.

If you are alone, you may think back and feel depressed. But when you are always busy with one thing or the other, you don't leave room for unnecessary thinking.

If you don't have anything to do, you can sleep. Proper sleep can help alleviate symptoms of depression to some extent.

Complete Detachment from the Past Relationship

When you still have items that will connect you with your past relationship, your healing may take time.

Forget about the past. You're free now!

Delete any kind of attachment with your ex, such as pictures or chats, and most especially pictures. Photos are taken to preserve memories. When you see pictures of when you were together with an ex, it will definitely make you feel sad, used, and betrayed.

This is not helping your healing in any way. Delete every picture or text that will refer you to the past.

Also, get rid of their number from your phone. Unfollow

them on Instagram, Facebook, Snapchat, and other social media platforms.

Just avoid anything that will trigger memories, and this will help speed up the healing process.

Patience is a Virtue

You need to know that this healing process will take a while. It doesn't just happen overnight. It is just like when someone is injured, and medication is required.

The wound does not heal immediately. It takes time before it does. Similarly with emotional wounds, you need to be patient. Gradually with all these things listed, you will heal and soon be back on your feet.

Although it may take time before everything goes back to normal, in the end, everything *will* be back to normal.

Do something productive

While in a relationship with a narcissist, you didn't really have time to do your thing. You were busy making your partner's needs your needs. Now that you are free from this nightmare, it is time to go back to that plan of yours.

Maybe you wanted to start a business, but you were unable to. It is time to work on it and do something productive. This will help speed up the process of healing.

Healing may take a few months or even a year, and leading a healthy and productive life after the abuse aids recovery. Many people have recovered from narcissistic abuse, and many others are still recovering from it.

Trust me, by doing all these five steps you'll soon be back in good shape. Know that you are not alone in this and you can power through this and get to the best days of your life.

Chapter 18

Healthy Love - Dating After a Narcissist

After surviving a nasty relationship with a narcissist, you begin to wonder whether you can ever love anyone in the way you loved your ex.

For the ladies, I am going to say, there are several good men out there that will treat you right in every possible way and the same goes for the men too. There are lots of single and healthy women out there in the world who are ready for love.

You just have to be patient and avoid falling into the hands of a narcissist.

At this point, I believe that you have learned so much from this book about who a narcissist is, and how to spot a narcissist on a first date and how to know if you are dealing with a narcissist right from the onset of a relationship. It shouldn't be hard for you to spot a narcissist. However, there are some covert narcissists, and you may not even know until you are deep into a relationship with them. So, do yourself a little favor by refreshing your mind about how to spot a covert narcissist as discussed earlier in the book.

This chapter will enlighten you on how to handle dating situations and find a non-toxic relationship, especially when you are fresh out of an abusive relationship. Let's dive in!

After surviving a narcissistic relationship, you have hopefully gone through some therapeutic sessions and you have also attended several support groups.

You even started a business, and now you are finally healed. All the pain and guilt is now in the past, and you're ready to move on with your life.

The chances are that you may want to get back out there in the dating game. It will be bad for anyone to advise you not to date again, because of one negative experience. But, to be sincere, there are so many good people out in the world waiting patiently for you to walk into their lives today.

All you have to do is put up some defenses that would ward off narcissists from you.

It is no new fact that after surviving an abusive relationship with a narcissist, you might be full of fears.

What if I met a narcissist again and I don't know?

What if he was really deceptive and I fall into his trap again?

You keep asking yourself so many *"what if?"* questions.

You are going to learn the tricks that can help you recognize toxic people early. When I say toxic people, I'm specifically talking about the narcissists and anyone who can hurt you.

The excellent first advice is to never rush into any relationship again. Pay more attention to the attitude of love interests and pay less to their looks but be discrete about it.

I mean, don't make it too visible. Narcissists may, on their first date with you, like to know more about you but say little about themselves. Make sure you ask your dates lots of questions, and when they try to dodge your questions, ensure they answer them.

When narcissists know all about you, they try to check out your weak points. Try not to disclose too much information too soon, just to be on the safer side.

Another essential key to recognizing anyone that is out to hurt is respect. What is meant by that? Anyone who doesn't respect you for who you are should not be in your life for any reason.

If you notice any little sign of disrespect, you need to bid them goodbye immediately. This time, you can't be waiting around for someone to hurt you again.

Another thing is that after healing, you need to set some standards for yourself. You need to have some kind of high esteem for yourself.

Know what you don't deserve or can't take and stand by your words. When you don't know your self-worth, that's when someone can treat you badly. By knowing your self-worth and establishing your standards, just anyone won't approach you. Knowing may not be convincing enough: you need some boldness and confidence to express yourself, either through your response or via your actions.

Let's assume you are a lady who has healed completely and you have decided to open up your heart again.

You met this guy who collected your digits, and you two started texting. You notice that all his talks were always leading to sex or mentioning sex.

You need to get your head together. He doesn't want to know you. He just wants sex. Forget the fact that you haven't had sex in a while. You need to protect yourself from men like this. Each time he says words like, "What are you doing at the moment?" or "would you like to come by the house this evening?" Be aware and careful! Don't allow anyone to play on your emotions anymore. Just say you're busy with something.

Maybe you met someone at a coffee shop, and you guys have started calling yourself and texting frequently. All of a sudden, he just disappears for a while. No calls, no text! Again, after a week, he resurfaces and texts you, "Hey beautiful, I missed you!" You need to run from that kind of person. There is a big possibility that the person is a narcissist. He doesn't mean what he said. He doesn't miss you.

It doesn't matter if he was a sweet guy before he ghosted you. When you reply to that kind of person, what you are telling them is that you have no self-worth or respect for yourself. They are going to continue treating you like that if you stay with them. Don't wait for him to start hurting you before you opt-out. Delete his digits and say your goodbye.

You are healed now, right? You are fresh and ready to mingle. You met this guy on tinder, and you gave him your number. One day he just calls you at night, asking you to come over to spend time with him. That's not appropriate. You are not sure about him yet. Just make up some excuse, that you are tired and you need to get up very early the next day. Wait for a little to see what he would say. If after giving that excuse, he still persists, then you know he doesn't care about you. He just wants to have his way with you. The question is, why didn't he ask you during the day time or make plans for earlier? Never answer to a late-night booty call, it just shows you have little esteem for yourself.

Again, you just met this great guy some days ago. Throughout the time you guys were chatting, he never mentioned that he was traveling or relocating to another city. He just called you that he was leaving the next day and that you should come over. He's not right for you! He's likely going to leave you after having his way with you. Don't fall for that! When this kind of thing happens, tell him that you are very busy with something and you won't be able to come to see him. Also, don't forget to wish him a safe trip if he calls you back after that day, then fine. If he doesn't, you just dodged a bullet. Most times, they never call back. They probably found someone else the trick worked on.

You may also meet some kind of guys who just want to see you without any planning. We've said earlier that you need to set some standards for yourself. That doesn't show he has any respect for you. What if you were busy and you couldn't make it? He doesn't care. Avoid this kind of person. Whenever you meet yourself in this kind of situation, say you are busy. Maybe, you could tell him you are free on the next Saturday. If he doesn't make an effort to plan a great time for you, he doesn't really care.

You have been talking to this guy you met at a business summit, and each time he tries to make plans with you, there is no certainty. He may say, "maybe we should go out this Thursday or Friday." Your reply should be that he should choose one because you are not sure you'll be available if he doesn't. Act like you have your own plans. He'll probably take it more seriously if he was actually into you. If he wasn't that into you, you might not hear from him again. He has to show some signs of commitment before you can accept his offer. This will show you are the kind of woman that can't be treated poorly.

If you are so important to him, he will value your time. Maybe, you made plans for dinner, and he's running late. If he doesn't call you to tell you he's running late, hop up and leave. On the second thought, if he calls you, tell him you have plans after dinner, and you may not be able to stay. Maybe you could fix another time! If he still came late, he doesn't feel you are good enough. Ditch him and move on. Don't let anyone waste your time. If he doesn't value your time, he doesn't value you at all. Don't start making unnecessary compromises when you've not even started dating. Remember that's how you got into that nasty relationship you had with your ex. You know better now!

From the beginning, right from little dates and

conversations, you need to be careful and notice every red flag that may lead to a nasty relationship. Set your boundaries, don't get too carried away with the outward looks, charming behavior, fame, charisma, and so on. Don't be overcommitted to someone; be ready to walk away at any time. Don't drop your future plans for anyone or change the direction of your life. Be as independent as possible. All these things may seem very rigid, but these are the precautions you must take to avoid falling into the wrong hands.

The same goes for men too, even if someone makes you feel important, still be patient enough to see it through. Don't be too quick to drop your defenses. Express your boundaries with subtlety and confidence without being angry. Most importantly, when you show people that you know you're worth, they will respect you. If they don't, you will know they are no good for you.

Chapter 19
First Date – How to Spot a Narcissist

HOW CAN YOU RECOGNIZE THE NARCISSIST FROM THE FIRST DATE?

No one deserves to be hurt or heartbroken, whether male or female. Being in a relationship with a narcissist, an egocentric, self-centered, and all-controlling person can be a horrible decision. Many women who have fallen victim of this kind of relationship always end up in bad shape after a crazy breakup.

If you are ignorant of who a narcissist is and how to spot them quickly, you will most likely fall under their trap. This chapter will enlighten you on how to recognize a narcissist right from the first date. I won't feed you with lies; identifying a narcissistic individual may be complicated. It takes a lot of focus and concentration to spot the difference. This is because they are highly skilled manipulators.

How does the Narcissist Appears on the First Date?

The first misconception I would like to correct is that some men may have a few qualities of a narcissist, but that doesn't mean they are. Having one or two conditions may not be harmful. Here, we want to help you dodge a bullet from the first date.

Narcissists are very confident people. Once they spot their prey, they make a move and can do anything in their power to get that person. They are really persuasive people. On your first date with a narcissist, he will appear very charming and 'too good' for you. Don't get me wrong, an average guy that really likes you can look this way too. There's something out of the ordinary when it comes to a narcissist. He could get a Lamborghini just to impress you. Just about anything to hook you. If you notice any 'too good to be true' kind of signs on your first date, that's a red flag.

Narcissists like to be in control of anything around them. They believe they are the best at everything. Let's say he planned dinner for two at a restaurant and you thought it was just something casual. A narcissist will dress to intimidate you in every way possible. He wants to show you that he is better than you. When you notice any of these red flags, you need to be more attentive to ascertain if he's a narcissist with other signs that you'll learn in this chapter.

What They Say

Another easy way to spot a narcissist on a first date is in what they say. From the way a person talks on the first date, you can deduce whether he's a narcissist or not. You just have to pay close attention. Narcissists are attention lovers; they'll do anything to keep the attention focused on them. They want everyone to know how successful they are. If on your first date, your date can't seem to stop talking about himself, that's a massive red flag. A narcissist will always try to direct all the attention to himself. They try to make each topic of discussion about them. If you notice this kind of attitude on your first date, there's no need for a second date.

Narcissists are good lovers on the first date. They are trying to win your heart, so they can come at you with different love quotes just to make you feel necessary. They can say, *"do you believe in love at first sight?"* Don't fall that easily! Wait for some other good signs before you jump into the wagon. Often times, toxic relationships are delightful in the beginning, especially on the first date. It could appear to be your best date since you've been dating. They could also say something like, *"we have so much in common."* Narcissists are cunning and manipulative. They ask a lot of questions on their first date with you just to know a lot about you. They want to know all about you but say little about themselves. Be careful! Do not reveal everything to them.

Lastly, narcissists always have a history of crazy exes. They may say, "my ex dumped me and left me heartbroken" or "my last few relationships have been awful." That's a durable quality of a narcissist. They never take the blame for anything, and they try their best to blame others. Narcissists are far from accountable or responsible for anything. When you notice that he keeps talking about what they did to him in his last relationships without having any fault whatsoever, that's a red flag.

The Signs Your Date Is a Narcissist

Here are a few reliable signs that your date is a narcissist:

The conversation

When on a date with someone, the primary purpose is to get to know each other, right? You bring up topics to be discussed by both parties. This is quite different from a narcissist. When on a date with a narcissist, the conversation becomes a monologue instead of a dialogue. He does all the talking, leaving little or no room for the other party to talk. They brag about themselves, their business, how they landed their first million, and so on.

Distraction

We said earlier that narcissists love attention, right? Each time you get distracted by something, they get really annoyed with you. They never want focus shifted away from them. They want to be the center of discussion; they want to be in control. Stay alert!

Special Treatment

Narcissists are so full of themselves. They have this belief that they should be treated specially. They plan your first date without acknowledging your opinion at all. On the first date, they may demand to change their sitting arrangements or quarrel with the waiter for something not worth it.

Impatient

Narcissists are very anxious individuals. They've no patience whatsoever. On your first date with a narcissist, he will most likely cause a scene with the manager of the restaurant he picked himself.

Critiques

One last thing you should look out for on your date is that narcissists are nasty critics. They are not satisfied with anything. They believe no one is better than them and what they are doing is the best.

How can you avoid the rest of the date?

After you've concluded that your date is a narcissist, you are halfway safe. What's remaining is how to avoid the remaining part of the date. Firstly, avoid feeding his ego by complimenting him on what he did or how he looks. Ask him a lot of questions and ensure he answers them. Make him feel intimidated and less in control. You can brag too, appear influential and highly esteemed. Try to disagree with whatever he says to you. Maybe he tells you very sweet and charming things; say something to counteract it. For instance, if he says something like, 'the first time I set my eyes on you...' try to say something mean that will make him feel you don't care. Deep down, narcissists are sad and low esteemed. If you make him think lesser than he feels or if he has no control at all over you, then you are free.

A lot has been said about narcissists, the red flags on a first date, how they appear, what they say, and how to avoid the rest of the date. It's better to avoid getting into a relationship with a monster at all from the first date. One thing you must be aware of is that it may not be easy spotting the signs discussed above in this chapter.

One needs to pay rapt attention to locate these few signs adequately. Some narcissists don't know they are narcissists and if you tell them, they will not agree with you. Rule out every notion to save them because you may end up getting heartbroken. Protect yourself first.

Conclusion

Thank you for coming this far. Narcissistic abuse does not only take place in personal and work relationships but also in contact with members of a community and even with public figures.

No matter whether it occurs on a personal or public level, it is vital to be aware of the signs of abuse as awareness of the negative situation is the first step to get out of it.

Narcissists are proud and self-centered individuals who lack empathy for others. They live in a world of their own making, and they believe that they are unique and special. Hence they always seek to serve their individual needs and won't mind using people as a means to further themselves

Many people have fallen victim to narcissistic abuse in general, and some have dated a narcissist or had an unhealthy relationship with one.

It is not a bad thing to seek love; in fact, one of the basic needs of humans is the need for a sense of belonging and acceptance by other people. There is nothing wrong in seeking love, but in the process of trying to find love, many have fallen victim to unhealthy relationships with abusive people.

Essential issues like identifying the behaviors of narcissists in dating, and learning how to deal with the narcissist who seeks control were discussed in full details. The stages of a typical relationship with a narcissist, Love-Bombing, Devaluing and Discarding, were discussed fully with real-life examples.

Why people fall victim to the wiles of the narcissist was not left out as the qualities that make people easy prey for the narcissists were extensively detailed. Psychological effects might linger for a very long time in the psyche of victims, even after they have quit the relationship with the narcissist and as such reading a material like this serves as a precaution not to fall victim to the narcissist's manipulative behavior.

Narcissists don't even think about how their behavior affects others, and this is why they find it so easy to use emotionally abusive and manipulative techniques in their relationships.

The previous chapters have revealed how narcissists operate in romantic relationships; it exposes the words they say and the actions they take to abuse victims.

Also, empowering strategies as to how to disarm narcissists and how to deal with narcissism in dating have been discussed.

Earlier on in the introduction, I promised you an informative and enlightening piece about dating a narcissist. I hope that the chapters of this book addressed every issue of concern of yours about dating a narcissist.

What I believe is that with the proper management techniques, any victim can get over the emotional abuse and mental manipulation of dating or being involved with a narcissist to go on and lead a productive and fulfilling life.

It is usual for victims of abuse to cry after their ordeal and think whatever went wrong with the relationship was their fault, which is what the narcissist wanted; a traumatic experience for the victim, and this book, I hope, has touched on everything needed for healing after dating a narcissist.

Do not read this alone and put it aside. Touch the lives of others with what you have learned, get copies for people you know are going through the ordeal and don't forget to provide all the support you can when you can.

Thank you, and good luck!

Printed in Great Britain
by Amazon